Jesus in the feasts of Israel

Richard Booker

Destiny Image Publishers
P.O. Box 351
Shippensburg, PA 17257
717-532-3040

Also by Richard Booker
available from Destiny Image Publishers:

Come and Dine
Intimacy with God
Miracle of the Scarlet Thread
Seated in Heavenly Places
Blow the Trumpet in Zion
Radical Christian Living
How to Prepare for the Coming Revival

JESUS IN THE FEASTS OF ISRAEL
© 1987 by Sounds of the Trumpet, Inc.
All Rights Reserved
Printed in the United States of America
Library of Congress Catalog Card Number: 87-71390

Destiny Image Publishers
P.O. Box 351
Shippensburg, PA 17257

ISBN 0-914903-98-5

For Worldwide Distribution
Printed in the U.S.A.

First printing: July 1987
Second printing: June 1989
Third printing: December 1990

Contents

Introduction

I'm sure you've heard the expression, "A picture is worth a thousand words." What is meant by this? Simply that we can more clearly communicate our thoughts with the use of visual aids than through words alone.

For example, if you want to teach a child the alphabet, you don't begin by giving that child a lecture on the theory of language. The child would not be able to comprehend what you were talking about. Instead, you give the child a block with a letter carved on it. The block is a visual aid to teach the child how to recognize a particular letter of the alphabet.

As the child learns, you give him or her more blocks with other letters until eventually the child has one block for each letter of the alphabet. Soon, the child is able to put these blocks together in correct sequence as they correspond to the alphabet and make up single words. The child has now learned the ABC's. Once this is accomplished, the blocks are no longer needed. They were temporary visual aids used as object lessons to teach the child the alphabet.

God's visual aids

As we can see in the Bible, God often used visual aids as object lessons to teach people specific truths He wanted them to understand. God used these visual aids in much the same manner that we would use the blocks to teach children

1

the alphabet. God has done this because in our fallen sinful nature, it is often difficult for us to understand spiritual truths. We perceive things through our physical senses much more clearly than we do through our spiritual senses.

In view of this, when God began to teach His covenant people, the Jews, He did so through the use of visual aids which the Jews could comprehend with their physical senses. God gave these visual aids in the Hebrew Scriptures (Old Testament part of the Bible) in the form of the various religious laws and rituals which the Jews were to observe. As the Jews practiced these laws and rituals, they would learn through their physical senses, spiritual truths concerning their relationship with God.

For 1,500 years, the Jewish people learned about God through their visual aids. Their religious laws and rituals taught them how to know God and walk with Him on a daily basis. But just as the child's blocks are not the real alphabet, neither were these physical pictures complete in themselves. They were only aids.

The ultimate visual aid

The time came when the Jews were to put away these physical symbols and enter into the spiritual reality which they portrayed. The transition from the physical to the spiritual was provided for them through the person and work of Jesus Christ, the Jewish Messiah and Savior of the world. This is what Jesus meant when He said, "Do not think that I have come to abolish the Law or the Prophets; I have not come to abolish them but to fulfill them" (Matthew 5:17, NIV).

We learn from this that the visual aids which God gave the Jewish people in the Hebrew Scriptures were given for the purpose of pointing them to their Messiah, Jesus. He was God's ultimate visual aid. Jesus said, "Anyone who has seen me has seen the Father" (John 14:9, NIV).

Now that Jesus has come, there is no need to seek God through religious rituals. We now have direct access to God through Christ. The rituals were only temporary visual aids. God used them as object lessons to teach the Jewish people about their coming Messiah. The apostle Paul was referring to this when he wrote, "Therefore the law was our tutor to bring us to Christ, that we might be justified [declared righteous] by faith. But after faith has come, we are no longer under a tutor" (Galatians 3:24-25, NKJV). We no longer need these rituals to show us the way to God. Jesus said, "I am the way, the truth, and the life. No one comes to the Father except through Me" (John 16:6, KJV).

This does not mean, however, that these Hebrew visual aids are no longer valuable to us. They still are very useful in helping us to better understand how to know God and walk with Him through a personal relationship with Jesus Christ. With an awareness of them, it is much easier to understand the New Testament Scriptures and the plan of God. They also have a prophetic significance and provide much insight concerning future events. For these reasons, Christians should be familiar with the Hebrew rituals and learn the spiritual truths they portray and how to apply those truths to our lives.

The Feasts of Jehovah

One of the clearest visual aids which God gave the Jews pertained to their religious holidays. The Bible refers to these religious holidays as the *Feasts of Jehovah*. God established these special celebrations when He brought the Hebrews out of Egypt. God spoke to Moses, saying, "Speak to the children of Israel, and say to them: 'The feast of the Lord, which you shall proclaim to be holy convocations, these are My feasts . . . These are the feasts of the Lord, holy convocations which you shall proclaim at their appointed times' " (Leviticus 23:2, 4, NKJV).

Today, when we hear the word "feast" we think of an elaborate meal or banquet. We tend to associate the word with food, but this is not the meaning of the word in this case. The Feasts of Jehovah were special holy convocations or assemblies established by God when the Jews would come together to meet God in a special way. They were religious gatherings. In this sense, Sunday church services for Christians are a type of feast because they are holy assemblies of God's people.

God established seven of these feasts and scheduled them on the Hebrew calendar in such a way that the Jews would have to travel to Jerusalem three times a year to keep them. These three feast seasons were known as Passover, Pentecost, and Tabernacles. They portrayed and represented three major encounters with God in the lives of His covenant people. These encounters with God were for the purpose of providing His divine peace, power, and rest in their lives (see Exodus 23:14-17; Deuteronomy 16:16).

The Feast of Passover was the first of these feast seasons. Its purpose was to teach the Hebrews how to find God's peace. Passover included the Feasts of Passover, Unleavened Bread, and First Fruits.

The next feast season was Pentecost. This was a single feast, and it taught the Hebrews how to receive God's power.

The third feast season was called Tabernacles. The purpose of the feast of Tabernacles was to teach the Hebrews how to enter God's rest, and included the feasts of Trumpets, Atonement, and Tabernacles.

The Feasts of Jehovah were very important visual aids for the Hebrew people. Each of the seven feasts pointed them to their Messiah, Jesus, and each uniquely portrayed a particular aspect of His life and ministry. Taken as a whole, they form a complete visual aid of the person and work of Jesus Christ, and the steps one must take to walk in the peace, power, and rest of God.

Why I wrote this book

Our world today is no different from the world of the Bible in that we all are still seeking peace. Nations are frantically seeking peace to avoid a nuclear holocaust. Individuals are seeking peace in their relationships. And personally we all are seeking peace within ourselves. The Bible says there will be no peace until man submits his life to God. Isaiah wrote, " 'There is no peace,' says the Lord, 'for the wicked' " (Isaiah 48:2, NKJV). The Feast of Passover teaches us how to have peace with God through Jesus Christ.

All who have acknowledged and received Jesus as their Lord and Savior have peace *with* God. But unfortunately not all followers of Jesus have the peace *of* God. Many Christians often are overcome by fear, worry, and anxiety. In the Feast of Passover, we learn not only how to have peace *with* God, but also the peace *of* God.

We not only need God's peace, we also need God's power. The Bible tells us that man is hopelessly enslaved to his own self-destructive habits. No matter how many New Year's resolutions we make, it seems we just are not able to keep them. Sin has a hold on us, and only God can set us free!

Psalms 62:11 says that power belongs to God. God has made His power available to us through Jesus Christ. Yet, not every Christian is walking in the power of Jesus. Many still are overcome by sin, Satan, and the fear of death. The Feast of Pentecost teaches us how to receive the power of God and appropriate it in our everyday lives.

We not only need God's peace and God's power, we also need God's rest. As the popular saying goes, "Life is not always a bowl of cherries." Our brief journey on earth is but a fleeting moment in which we constantly war against the attacks of the world on our soul. Things don't always turn out the way we hoped they would. Life is full of disappointments, heartaches, burdens, and trials. Even Christians sometimes grow weary in trying to serve God and cope with the struggles of life. The Feast of Tabernacles teaches us how to enter into the rest of God.

I'm sure we will all agree that the above mentioned considerations are life's most difficult challenges. Yet, God has provided a means for us to live victoriously in them through Jesus Christ. I wrote this book to help you learn how to encounter God in such a way that you will walk in His divine peace, power, and rest.

A look at what's ahead

You'll begin in chapter two with a brief look at the Jewish calendar. You might well ask, "What in the world does the Jewish calender have to do with my having peace, power, and rest of God?" The connection, simply, is that God established these feasts on the Jewish calendar to be celebrated at a certain time and in a certain sequence.

The reason God did this was that Jesus Christ was to fulfill them in His own life and ministry on the exact dates that the Jews had been celebrating them for 1,500 years. Jesus fulfilled the first two feast seasons (Passover and Pentecost) at His first coming. He will fulfill the third feast season (Tabernacles) at His second coming. So there is a tremendous amount of prophetic significance in the Jewish calendar. The time and sequence of these feasts reveal the overall prophetic plan of God.

From a personal standpoint, it is helpful to understand the Jewish calendar for the purpose of learning how to apply the spiritual truths portrayed in the feasts to your own life.

Then in chapters two through eight, we'll study each feast in detail. We'll look back into the Hebrew Scriptures and see exactly what God told the Jews to do and how they celebrated each feast. Then we will look into the New Testament and discover how Jesus fulfilled the feast. After making this connection, you'll learn how to apply what Jesus accomplished to your own life. Finally, you'll see how God has been restoring the spiritual realities of these feasts throughout the history of the Church.

In addition, there is a review exercise at the end of each of the chapters to help you highlight and reinforce what you learned. The review exercises may be completed on an individual or group basis.

As you continue to read, may God bless you with a special awareness of His presence and help you to walk in His peace, power, and rest.

Introduction
Review Exercise

1. Why does God use visual aids to teach us spiritual truths?

2. Why is it helpful for Christians to understand the Hebrew rituals?

3. What are the Feasts of Jehovah?

4. Name the three feast seasons, and state briefly the spiritual significance of each.
   a.

   b.

   c.

1
the Jewish calender

The standarized calendar used by the world today is known as the Gregorian calendar. This calendar gets its name from Pope Gregory XIII who established it in 1582. This is a sun or "solar" calendar due to the fact that it operates on the principle of the earth revolving around the sun. The different seasons we enjoy are caused by the changing position of the earth as it makes it course around the sun.

As we know, the days on this calendar begin at midnight and last for 24 hours. It takes approximately 365¼ days for the earth to make a complete circle around the sun. This is how we determine the length of the year on the Gregorian calendar. However, some adjustment must be made for the extra quarter of a day. This is why an extra day is added every four years making a Leap Year of 366 days.

The Jewish calendar is a moon or "lunar" calendar based on the movement of the moon around the earth. The days on this calendar begin at sundown (approximately 6:00 P.M.) and also lasts for 24 hours. It takes approximately 29½ days for the moon to make a complete circle around the earth. Twelve of these lunar months add up to about 354 days in a lunar year.

Notice that the solar year is 11¼ days longer than the lunar year. This difference requires the Jews to make adjustments to their calendar or else after a few years, they would be celebrating their feast days in the wrong season of the year. God set fixed times and seasons when the Jews were to keep their feasts (Leviticus 23:4). For example, He told them to celebrate the Feast of Passover during the spring time of the year. If the Jews did not periodically adjust their calendar, they would miss spring by an additional 11¼ days each year. So that after five years, for example, they would be celebrating Passover 56¼ days late and completely out of season.

To compensate for this yearly difference of 11¼ days, the Jewish calendar also has a Leap Year. Instead of adding an extra day every fourth year as on the Gregorian calendar, they add an extra month at the end of every third year. This month is called the intercalary month. It is 29 days long and makes up most of the difference between the two calendars. This adjustment enables the Jews to keep their feast days in the seasons called for by the Bible.

Let's now take a look at the Jewish calendar for the purpose of getting a basic understanding of how it is organized. A copy of the calendar is provided at the end of this chapter. You will need to refer to it for this discussion.

The sacred calendar

Notice that the Jews had two concurrent calendar years. One was a sacred calendar year which God established when He brought them out of Egypt. In Exodus 12:2 God told them that their deliverance from Egypt was to be the beginning of their sacred calendar and that Nisan would be the first month of the year of this calendar. This month originally was called Abib, but later was changed to Nisan during the Babylonian captivity. Observe that Nisan corresponds to the months of March and April on the Gregorian calendar. Each Hebrew month may come in one or two Gregorian months because of the 11¼ days difference between the calendars.

The civil calendar

The other calendar year was a civil calendar based on the Jews' agricultural season. The civil calendar begins with the month of Tishri, which corresponds to the months of September and October, and is the beginning of the agricultural season.

The civil calendar and agricultural season began with the early rains that softened the ground for plowing which was done in October and November. This was followed by the sowing of the wheat and barley seed in November and December. The winter rains came in December and January to keep the ground moist. This was followed by the blossoming of the almond trees in January and February, and the citrus harvest in February and March.

The spring or latter rains fell in March and April concurrent with the beginning of the barley harvest. The dry season was from April and May to September and October. The barley harvest lasted through the spring months and was followed by the wheat harvest in May and June. The grape harvest came next during the months of June and July. July and August was the time of the olive harvest. August and September brought the season to a close with the harvest of dates and figs.

The feast seasons

Passover was the first feast celebrated and represented the first of the three major encounters with God in the lives of His covenant people. For this reason, the sacred calendar begins with Passover in the month of Nisan (March-April), which was celebrated during the barley harvest. These feast seasons were physical symbols showing

11

the Jews how to know God and walk with Him through a personal relationship with Jesus. The spiritual truths symbolized by the feasts are available to all who will turn to God through Jesus as their Lord and Savior. The very first encounter we have with God through Jesus brings us forgiveness of sin and reconciliation with our Creator-God. The result is that we have peace *with* God and the peace *of* God. For this reason, the Feast of Passover is the first feast celebrated on the sacred Jewish calendar.

The Feast of Pentecost was celebrated next because it represented the second major encounter with God which is His power. Every person needs the power of God working in their life. Once we have peace with God through Jesus, we can then experience His power. For this reason, the Feast of Pentecost was the second feast celebrated on the Jewish sacred calendar. It came at the time of the wheat harvest in the month of Sivan (May-June).

The Feast of Tabernacles was celebrated last at the very end of the agricultural season and the beginning of the new one. This was during the Hebrew month of Tishri (September-October). God placed it in this position on the sacred Jewish calendar because it represented His third and last encounter in the lives of His people. This final encounter with God represents that place in our walk with God where we enter into His divine rest. God's peace comes first, then His power, then His rest.

A study of the Jewish calendar is certainly not important in itself. Our knowledge of it is only for the purpose of understanding God's plan of salvation for man through the person and work of Jesus Christ. As we study these feasts in the next chapters, we'll see very clearly that God does have a plan for redeeming all who will come to Him through Jesus Christ.

Through our study of the feasts, we'll learn that God's

plan for working out His redemption has a definite beginning, a definite process, and a definite conclusion. This relates not only to the person and work of Jesus Christ, but also to the lives of individual believers in their walk with God and the establishing of the kingdom of God on the earth.

JEWISH CALENDAR

Sacred	Civil	Name of Months	Farm Season	Feast
1	7	Nisan — Mar–Apr	Barley Harvest	Passover
2	8	Iyyar — Apr–May	Barley Harvest	
3	9	Sivan — May–Jun	Wheat Harvest	Pentecost
4	10	Tammuz — Jun–Jul	Grape Harvest	
5	11	Ab — Jul–Aug	Olive Harvest	
6	12	Elul — Aug–Sep	Dates–Figs Harvest	
7	1	Tishri — Sep–Oct	Early Rains	Tabernacles
8	2	Heshvan — Oct–Nov	Plowing	
9	3	Kieslev — Nov–Dec	Wheat–Barley Sowing	
10	4	Tebeth — Dec–Jan	Winter Rains	
11	5	Shebat — Jan–Feb	Almond Bloom	
12	6	Adar — Feb–Mar	Citrus Harvest	
			(Latter Rains)	
13	—	Adar Sheni	Intercalary Month	

Chapter One
Review Exercise

1. What is the difference between the Jewish calendar and the standardized calendar used by the world?

2. Name the two concurrent calendar years used by the Jews.
   a.

   b.

3. List the three feast seasons in the order in which they were celebrated.
   a.

   b.

   c.

2

passover

A chart entitled *The Feasts of the Lord* is provided at the end of this chapter. This chart highlights the main aspects of each feast and will help you understand more clearly the teachings in this book. You should refer to it as we discuss the individual feasts in detail in each chapter.

As you look at the chart, notice there are six columns, each with their respective heading. The first two columns are provided for the purpose of helping you to become familiar with when the feasts are celebrated. The farming season and respective Hebrew months are shown along with the specific dates on which the feasts were celebrated.

The next four columns show the four aspects that we will be discussing for each. They are the main focus of this book. In the first column, we will discuss the historical aspect of the feast. We will do this by examining the instructions God gave the Jews in the Old Testament for celebrating the feast. Then we'll look into the New Testament and see how Jesus fulfilled the spiritual reality that the feast symbolized. Next, we'll learn how to apply this work of Jesus to our own life. This is the personal application and represents the seven steps to Christian maturity and God's rest. Finally, we'll consider the seasonal aspect of the feast which will show us their prophetic significance and how God brings the truths portrayed by these feasts to the Church. Let's begin now with Passover.

Historical background

Passover was the first of the three feast seasons. All Jewish males were required to journey to Jerusalem for a special encounter with and visitation from God. It was celebrated during the barley harvest in the month of Nisan and included the three feasts of Passover, Unleavened Bread, and First Fruits.

The instructions for celebrating the feasts are found throughout the Old Testament. Leviticus 23 provides a good summary of them all. Numbers 28-29 and Deuteronomy 16 also provide a good summary.

Let's now consider the historical aspects of Passover. It states in Leviticus, "These are the feasts of the LORD, holy convocations which you shall proclaim at their appointed times [in their seasons]. 'On the fourteenth day of the first month at twilight [evening] is the LORD'S Passover' " (Leviticus 23:4-5, NKJV).

The Passover was to be a memorial to the Hebrews' deliverance from Egypt. This deliverance happened during the month of Nisan and represented God's first encounter with His covenant people.

God chose Moses as His instrument to lead the Hebrews out of bondage. Working through Moses, God sent ten terrible plagues against Egypt. This was God's way of convincing Pharaoh to let the Hebrews go. But each time God sent a new plague, Pharaoh's heart hardened (Exodus 3-10).

God gave Pharaoh every chance to let the Hebrews go, but Pharaoh would not yield. God then declared a tenth and final plague which was the death of the firstborn of every family (Exodus 11). But along with this decree of death, God gave specific instructions on how to be saved from this death.

The complete record of this culminating event which resulted in the Hebrew deliverance from Egypt is recorded in the book of Exodus. If you have a Bible, I would suggest you take a moment and read that account before continuing with this chapter. The specific Scriptures to read are Exodus 12:1-14, 43-48.

Let's summarize what God said for the purpose of spotlighting certain key points of His instructions. Every man was to select for his household a lamb without spot or blemish. He was to select this lamb on the tenth day of the month. Then he was to observe this lamb for five days to make sure there was nothing wrong with him. There could be no fault (spot or blemish) found in this lamb.

On the fifth day, he was to bring the lamb to his doorstep and kill him. As he killed the animal, he would catch the blood in the basin at the foot of the doorstep. Then he would sprinkle the blood on both sides of the doorpost and above the doorpost. Thus, the entire entrance into the house was covered by the blood of the lamb.

This was to be done on the evening of the fourteenth (twilight). We're already mentioned that the Hebrew day begins in the evening at approximately six o'clock. The Hebrews killed the lambs at three o'clock in the afternoon on the fourteenth in order to eat the meal by six. When three o'clock arrived, they slaughtered the lambs and applied the blood to their doorpost. The family then entered their house through the blood-stained door where they were protected from the plague of death that was to move through the land.

According to the instructions, the entire lamb was to be roasted and consumed. Nothing could be left over for the next day. In preparing the meal, not one bone of the lamb was to be broken. To roast a lamb according to these instructions required that the lamb be placed on a spit shaped like a crossbar so that its body could be spread open.

Although the family went inside the house and couldn't see the blood covering, they had faith that God would save them because of it. As they ate their meal, God allowed the angel of death to sweep through the land. As he passed from door to door he sought to enter every household. If the entrance was covered by blood, the angel of death could not enter but had to *pass over* that house. The blood was a seal protecting the people inside. However, if the entrance was not covered by blood, judgment would come upon that household as the firstborn would die.

This was the Lord's Passover. And we see that He used the blood of the lamb to save His people from death. The blood of the lamb made atonement for their sins and was God's way of saving His covenant people.

God further instructed that no uncircumcized person could partake of the Passover meal or celebrate the feast. The significance of this was that circumcision was the outward evidence that the person was in covenant with God. It showed that the individual had accepted the Hebrew God as the one true God and had entered into a blood covenant with Him.

Thus, if a Gentile came to accept the Hebrew God for himself, he had to be circumcised. He would then be considered as one born in the land. This means that he would be an heir to the promises made to Abraham and could inherit the blessings that were part of God's covenant with the Jewish people.

Later when the Temple was built, instead of killing the lambs at the doorpost, the people would bring the lambs to Jerusalem and kill them at the Temple.

The Passover celebration was a time of great joy, praise, and adoration in worship to God. As they sacrificed at the Temple, the Levites would lead the people in singing the Psalms of David. They specifically sang Psalms 113-118. They began by all singing the first line of each Psalm. Then the Levites would sing the second line of each Psalm and the people would respond by saying "Hallelujah" or "Praise ye the Lord."

The singing was accompanied with musical instruments of trumpets, harps, flutes, tamborines, the cymbals, and other instruments. It reached its peak as those who were present lifted their voices to God and sang, "This is the day the Lord hath made; we will rejoice and be glad in it" (see Psalms 118:24).

As time passed, however, it became more difficult for the people in the outlying areas to bring their sacrifice to Jerusalem. So the Levites began raising lambs for the Passover sacrifice right in Jerusalem and selling them at the Temple.

Then when the Hebrews came to Jerusalem to celebrate Passover, they could buy a lamb already set aside for sacrifice. It was a lamb that had been closely inspected and without spot or blemish. It was a lamb that they found no fault in but it was born to die as a Passover lamb.

How Jesus fulfilled

For 1,500 years the Jews had been celebrating the Feast of Passover by killing a lamb and offering it as a sacrifice to God. They knew about lambs. But the blood of an animal could only *cover* their sins, it could not take them away. In view of this, God raised up prophets to explain to the people that, one day in the future, a human lamb would come who would deal with the problem of sin and death once and for all.

The prophet Isaiah spoke of the suffering this human lamb would experience. He wrote a very clear, vivid description which is recorded for us in Isaiah, chapter 53. It would be helpful to read that entire chapter as part of this study.

As the time came for this human lamb to be sacrificed, God sent one last prophet to help the people recognize Him. This prophet was John the Baptist, the forerunner of Jesus. John introduced Jesus with these words, "Behold! The Lamb of God who takes away the sin of the world" (John 1:29 NKJV)! The following day, John again saw Jesus and repeated this startling introduction, "Behold the Lamb of God" (John 1:36, NKJV)!

John identified Jesus as the human lamb Isaiah spoke of who would give His life for the sins of the world. For this purpose, Jesus was born (Acts 2:22-23). Because of their religious sacrifices, the Jews immediately understood the significance of John's statements concerning Jesus.

You will notice in the accompanying chart that Jesus fulfilled the Feast of Passover in His crucifixion. Since this was the reason for Him being born, Jesus' entire life was predestined so that He would fulfill this purpose exactly as God had instructed the Jews to practice it for 1,500 years.

In view of this, as the time approached for Jesus to die, He deliberately arranged His itinerary and personal activities around the events associated with the selection, testing, and death of the Passover lamb. In this way, the Jewish people would be able to understand who He was and what He was doing. Jesus was set aside to be sacrificed, examined and crucified on the exact month, day, and hour that the Jews had been handling the lambs for 1,500 years in keeping the Feast of Passover.

Let's now see this for ourselves in the New Testament. When God established the Passover feast in Egypt, He instructed the Jews to set aside their lambs on the tenth day of the month of Nisan. In the New Testament we learn that it was the tenth day of the month of Nisan when Jesus entered Jerusalem to be set aside as the human lamb.

In John 12:1 we find that Jesus came to the town of Bethany six days before the Passover. John writes, "Then, six days before the Passover, Jesus came to Bethany" (John 12:1, NKJV). Since Passover was celebrated on the fourteenth, this would mean that Jesus came to Bethany on the ninth.

John then gives us further information to show us that the ninth was on a Saturday. He goes on to say, "The next day a great multitude that had come to the feast, when they heard that Jesus was coming to Jerusalem, took branches of palm trees and went out to meet Him, and cried out: 'Hosanna! "Blessed is He who comes in the name of the LORD!" The king of Israel' " (John 12:12-13, NKJV).

John says that it was the next day when Jesus rode into Jerusalem and was greeted by the cheering crowds. This, of course, is what the Christian church has historically referred to as Palm Sunday. From this, we learn that Jesus was in Bethany on Saturday, the ninth of Nisan. The next day was Sunday, the tenth of Nisan. Jesus entered Jerusalem to be set aside as the human lamb of God on the exact date that God told the Jews to set aside their lambs back in Egypt.

The purpose for setting aside the lamb, as we've mentioned, was to observe him to make sure he was without spot or blemish. This lamb was to be offered to God. God is perfect. You wouldn't offer a lamb to God that was blemished. So the Jews observed and tested the lamb for five days to make sure that it was faultless.

Likewise, Jesus, the human lamb was observed and tested for five days by the religious leaders. They questioned His authority (Matthew 21:23-27). They asked Him trick questions hoping He would somehow give a wrong answer which they could use against Him (Matthew 23). They did everything they could to point an accusing finger at Him and discredit Him so that He would not be an acceptable sacrifice.

But Jesus always responded to them perfectly. They could not find anything wrong with Him. Finally in desperation, they took Jesus to the Roman governor, whose name was Pilate, hoping he could find something wrong with Jesus. But after interrogating and beating Jesus, Pilate said of Him, "I find no fault in Him" (John 19:4, NKJV). This all happened in the five-day period from the tenth to the fourteenth when the Jews were checking their lambs for sacrifice.

And finally, Jesus was crucified on the fourteenth. He was not only crucified on the same day the lambs were killed, but also at the same time of day.

Jesus said to His disciples, "You know that after two days is the Passover, and the Son of Man will be delivered up to be crucified" (Matthew 26:2, NKJV). We know from God's instructions in the Hebrew Scriptures that Passover was on the fourteenth of Nisan. Jesus tells His disciples that He will be crucified on Passover. By a simple calculation, we learn that this was on a Thursday, since the previous Sunday when Jesus rode into Jerusalem was on the tenth.

Josephus, a first century Jewish historian, reported that there were about 256,500 lambs killed in Jerusalem the year Jesus was crucified. With this many lambs, it was necessary for the Jews to prepare them for sacrifice at nine o'clock in the morning on the fourteenth. They then killed them at three o'clock that afternoon so that the Passover could be completed before six o'clock which would begin a new day.

At the exact hour when the Jews were preparing their lambs for sacrifice, Jesus was nailed to the cross. Mark wrote, "Now it was the third hour, and they crucified Him"

(Mark 15:25, NKJV). The third hour was nine o'clock in the morning, Jewish time.

In fulfillment of the Feast of Passover and Isaiah's prophecy, Jesus bore our griefs and carried our sorrows. He was wounded for our transgressions and bruised for our iniquities. The Lord God laid on Jesus the iniquity of us all. He was oppressed and afflicted. Yet He opened not His mouth, like a lamb led to the slaughter.

Then at three o'clock as the people were praising God and slaughtering the lambs, Jesus died. Mark was careful to note the time and wrote that it was the ninth hour (three o'clock Jewish time) when Jesus breathed His last breath (see Mark 15:33-37).

Jesus gave His total self to be roasted and consumed in the judgment fires of God as He died for our sins. The spit on which the lambs were spread open was shaped like a crossbar and pointed to Jesus hanging on the cross.

All the other details concerning the death of the lambs happened to Jesus—the real Lamb of God. For example, His bones were not broken. Remember, God said not to break any bones in the Passover lamb (Exodus 12:46; Numbers 9:12; Psalms 34:20).

When a person is crucified, his body sags so that he cannot breathe. This causes him to push himself up with his heel just long enough to take a deep breath. To hasten the person's death, the Roman soldier would break his legs, thus, he would not be able to push himself up to get air.

John records that the soldiers broke the legs of the two thieves who were crucified next to Jesus. But when they came to Jesus, they saw that He already was dead and did not break His legs (John 19:31-33). John saw this and wrote, "For these things were done that the Scripture should be fulfilled, 'Not one of His bones shall be broken' " (John 19:36, NKJV).

25

God had specifically instructed the Jews to consume the whole lamb. Nothing was to be left over for the next day (Exodus 12:10). This also was the case with Jesus. The Jews, not realizing they were carrying out God's plan, hurriedly had Jesus' body taken down before six o'clock.

John wrote, "Therefore, because it was the Preparation Day, that the bodies should not remain on the cross on the Sabbath (for that Sabbath was a high day), the Jews asked Pilate that their legs might be broken, and that they might be taken away" (John 19:31, NKJV). Jesus, the Sacrificial Lamb, was not left on the cross the next day but gave His all on the fourteenth as the final Passover sacrifice.

The blood of the Passover lamb was a visual aid directing the Hebrew into the future when Jesus would come and establish the spiritual reality that the lambs could only symbolize. The blood of Jesus saves us from death.

Peter wrote, "knowing that you were not redeemed with corruptible things, like silver or gold, from your aimless conduct received by tradition from your fathers, but with the precious blood of Christ, as of a lamb without blemish and without spot. He indeed was foreordained before the foundation of the world, but was manifest in these last times for you who through Him believe in God, who raised Him from the dead and gave Him glory, so that your faith and hope are in God" (1 Peter 1:18-21, NKJV).

The apostle Paul made this connection when he stated, "For indeed Christ, our Passover, was sacrificed for us" (1 Corinthians 5:7, NKJV).

Personal application

Let's now look at the personal application this feast has for us today. The Bible says that all of us have sinned and that the penalty for our sin is death (Romans 3:23; 6:23). As with the Hebrews back in Egypt, the angel of death comes

26

knocking at our door. The writer of Hebrews tells us that the great hold which Satan has on humanity is the fear of death (Hebrews 2:14-15). Death is the one subject we don't like to think or talk about.

Not only are we afraid of death, but we're also afraid of God. We're afraid of God because deep down inside we know we're sinners and that our sins have separated us from God. We know that God would be perfectly just in punishing us. So we run from God. We try to hide from Him behind the walls of religion, business, power, money, fame, glamour, success, etc. We keep ourselves busy, and numb our minds in order not to think about Him. Repeating Isaiah's words, " 'there is no peace,' says the LORD, 'for the wicked' " (Isaiah 48:2, NKJV).

Even though we deserve death, God has made a way for us to be saved. That way is through the blood of Jesus Christ which cleanses us from all sin (1 John 1:7). When we apply it to the doorpost of our heart, death cannot hold us. We no longer need to fear death because the resurrection of Jesus Christ has taken away its sting (see 1 Corinthians 15:51-57).

The same is true for our fear of God. We no longer have to run from God when we accept the Lord Jesus Christ as the Lamb of God who died for our sins. God accepts Jesus' death in our place. He is our innocent substitutionary sacrifice. We are reconciled to God when we acknowledge Jesus as the one who died on our behalf.

Paul wrote, "But now in Christ Jesus you who once were far off have been made near by the blood of Christ" (Ephesians 2:13, NKJV). This means there is no condemnation for those who come to Christ (Romans 8:1). We shall not come into condemnation for we have passed from death to life (John 5:24).

The result of our coming to Christ as our Passover sacrifice is peace with God. We read these words in Romans,

"Therefore, having been justified by faith, we have peace with God through our Lord Jesus Christ . . . But God demonstrated His own love toward us, in that while we were still sinners, Christ died for us. Much more then, having now been justified by His blood, we shall be saved from wrath through Him" (Romans 5:1, 8-9, NKJV).

Accepting Jesus Christ as our Lord and Savior is the first major encounter we have with God. This is how we find peace with God. This is what the Feast of Passover symbolized.

The first of the seven steps to know God and walk with Him is to accept Jesus Christ as our personal Lord and Savior and thereby experience a spiritual new birth.

God told the Hebrews that no uncircumcised person could celebrate the Passover feast nor the Passover meal. As I have pointed out, circumcision was the outward evidence that the person was in covenant with God. If a person accepted circumcision, it showed that he recognized the Hebrew God as his own God. This enabled him to receive the blessings that were part of God's covenant with the Jewish people.

But God was interested in something much greater than just a cutting of the flesh. He wanted the people to have a circumcised heart. He said, "Therefore circumcise the foreskin of your heart, and be stiff-necked no longer" (Deuteronomy 10:16, NKJV). Jeremiah added, "Circumcise yourselves to the LORD, And take away the foreskins of your hearts" (Jeremiah 4:4, NKJV).

We become children of God by faith in Jesus Christ which is evidenced, not by a circumcision of the flesh, but a circumcision of the heart (Galatians 3:26). Jesus spoke of this as being born again (see John 3:1-7). This is a spiritual rebirth that takes place the moment we accept Jesus as our Passover Lamb and ask Him to come into our life. Jesus gives us the Holy Spirit who comes to live in us changing our heart and making us a new creation in Christ. This is what God had in mind all along. Physical circumcision was just a symbol of the true circumcision which is of the Spirit.

Paul often contrasted physical and spiritual circumcision pointing out the inadequacy of the old and the necessity of the new. He said, "For we are the circumcision, who worship God in the Spirit, rejoice in Christ Jesus, and have no confidence in the flesh" (Philippians 3:3, NKJV). "For he is not a Jew who is one outwardly, nor is that circumcision which is outward in the flesh; but he is a Jew who is one inwardly, and circumcision is that of the heart, in the Spirit" (Romans 2:28-29, NKJV). "For in Christ Jesus neither circumcision nor uncircumcision avails anything, but a new creation" (Galatians 6:15, NKJV). "Therefore, if anyone is in Christ, he is a new creation; old things have passed away; behold all things have become new" (2 Corinthians 5:17, NKJV).

Seasonal aspect

God instructed the Hebrews to keep the feasts in their seasons (Leviticus 23:4). By this, of course, He meant the agricultural seasons. God also has prophetic seasons. God's prophetic seasons are those periods of time in world history when God moves to establish and restore the spiritual meanings of these feasts in the lives of His covenant people, be they Jew or Gentile. These are major moves of God that affect the whole world but particularly the Jewish people and the universal Church of Jesus Christ.

You'll notice from the chart that the seasonal aspect of Passover is connected with Martin Luther. For centuries, the biblical truth symbolized by the Feast of Passover was not clearly taught by the religious leaders of the Church. This came about in the following way.

In A.D. 312, the Emperor Constantine decreed that Christianity was to be the official religion of Rome. But, of course, no one can decree that another person become a Christian. Christianity is a matter of the heart. But the people had to outwardly obey even though inwardly most never actually accepted Jesus personally and experienced the new birth. Rome embraced Christianity, but the Romans themselves did not become Christians. People joined a religious system, but they never had a change on the inside.

During the next 1,200 years, many unbiblical practices were taught by the institutional church. Church leaders did not clearly teach the biblical declaration that salvation is based on a personal relationship with Jesus Christ, and the necessity of the new birth. The significance of the Feast of Passover was unknown to the common man. People sought salvation through religious rituals rather than through personal faith in Jesus Christ as their human Passover Lamb.

In the 1500's, God raised up Martin Luther to restore the meaning of the Feast of Passover to the Christian world. At the age of 22, Luther was knocked to the ground by a bolt of lightning during a terrible thunderstorm. Because his life was spared, Luther made a vow to become a monk. He was ordained in 1507 and after studying theology, he taught religion at the University of Wittenberg.

Because of his theological orientation, Luther tried to find peace with God through the rituals and traditions of the church. He kept them all, as best a man could, with great zeal and devotion. He fasted, he prayed, he confessed his sins, he appealed to the saints and the virgin Mary for help. He forsook all creature comforts and submitted his body to the most primitive conditions in an attempt to gain favor with God and overcome temptation. His failures to find God through these outward works left him empty, confused, and frustrated.

In the year 1515, Luther devoted himself to studying Paul's letter to the Romans. It was during this study that Luther came to realize that salvation was not based on religious acts or outward works, but was a free gift from God available through personal faith in Jesus Christ. The particular verse that God used to open Luther's eyes was Romans 1:17 which says, ". . . the just shall live by faith" (NKJV).

With this fresh understanding of God's Word, Luther became a changed man. He put his personal faith in Jesus Christ as the Passover Lamb who had died for his sins. He became a new creation in Christ and was born again by the Spirit of God. The whole of Scripture took on new meaning for Luther. He proclaimed his new understanding with a boldness that shook the world.

God used Luther to restore to the Church the truth of the Feast of Passover as it was fulfilled in Jesus Christ. In 1517, he protested the church's sale of indulgences which triggered the Protestant Reformation and changed the course of history.

THE FEASTS OF THE LORD

Farming Season	Hebrew Month	Feast (Historical)	Jesus (Prophetic)	Believer (Personal)	Seasonal (Seasonal)
Barley Harvest	Nisan 14 15-21 17	**Passover** Passover Unleavened Bread Firstfruits	Crucified Buried Resurrected	New Birth Put Off Old Put On New	Luther–1517 Wesley–1738
	Iyyar	50 Days From Resurrection To Pentecost			
Wheat Harvest	Sivan 6	**Pentecost**	Exalted	Baptism In Holy Spirit	Kansas–1901 Los An.–1906
Fruit Harvest	Tammuz Ab Elul	No Feast—The Church Period			
Final Ingathering	Tishri 1 10 15-21	**Tabernacles** Trumpets Day Of Atonement Tabernacles	Defeating Enemy Purifying Bride Coming Again	Full Armor Baptism In Fire God's Rest	Present Future Future

Nisan —Mar-Apr
Iyyar —Apr-May
Sivan —May-Jun

Tammuz —Jun-Jul
Ab —Jul-Aug
Elul —Aug-Sep

Tishri —Sep-Oct

Chapter Two
Review Exercise

1. Describe how Jesus fulfilled the Feast of Passover.

2. How does the Feast of Passover through Jesus apply to our lives today?

3. Describe the seasonal aspect of the Feast of Passover.

3
unleavened bread

The Feast of Passover, as fulfilled in Jesus Christ, affects your position before God. Prior to receiving Jesus as your personal Savior, your sins separate you from God. But once you accept Jesus as the Passover Lamb of God who died for your sins, your position before God changes. Something wonderful happens! God declares you "not guilty."

This change in your position before God is called "justification" (see Romans 3:24, 26, 28; 4:5, 25; 5:1, 9; 8:30, Galatians 2:16). It is a judicial act of God regarding your position before Him. In justifying you, God imputes or credits the perfect righteousness of Jesus Christ to your spiritual bank account.

This is what Paul was speaking of when he wrote, "For He [God] made Him [Jesus] who knew no sin to be sin for us, that we might become the righteousness of God in Him" (2 Corinthians 5:21, NKJV).

God declares us to be righteous through Jesus Christ. This is wonderful news and cause for rejoicing. We no longer feel we must run from God and bear the burden of guilt for our sins. God has forgiven our sins and no longer remembers them. He has separated us from them as far as the east is from the west. He has cast them into the sea of forgetfulness. We have peace with God. This is indeed the Good News!

But there is more. This is just the beginning of an adventurous walk with God. For God is not only interested in our position, He's also interested in our condition. God not only cares about what you *were* and what you're *going to be,* He also cares about what you are *now!* God wants to change your life and transform you into the moral image and character of Jesus Christ, beginning right now.

God established the Feasts of Unleavened Bread and First Fruits as visual aids for the purpose of teaching us how He desires to change our condition through Jesus Christ. Both of these feasts are concerned with our condition before God.

Historical background

God gives the following instructions concerning the Feast of Unleavened Bread, "And on the fifteenth day of the same month is the Feast of Unleavened Bread to the LORD; seven days you must eat unleavened bread. On the first day you shall have a holy convocation; you shall do no customary work on it. But you shall offer an offering made by fire to the LORD for seven days. The seventh day shall be a holy convocation; you shall do no customary work on it" (Leviticus 23:6-8, NKJV).

The Feast of Unleavened Bread was celebrated the day after Passover and lasted from the fifteenth to the twenty-first in the Hebrew month of Nisan.

When God delivered the Hebrews from Egypt, He brought them out with such haste that they did not have time to cook their bread which would normally have included leaven. Leaven became symbolic of the Hebrew's old life of bondage in Egypt under Pharaoh and the Egyptian's world system. Unleavened bread symbolized their putting off this old life as they came out of Egypt.

36

God instructed the Hebrews to keep the Feast of Unleavened Bread as a memorial to their separation from Egypt. Unleavened bread was not eaten at Passover on the fourteenth nor for the next seven days, as it is stated in Exodus 13:3-7, "Remember this day in which you went out of Egypt, out of the house of bondage; for by strength of hand the LORD brought you out of this place. No leavened bread shall be eaten . . . Unleavened bread shall be eaten seven days. And no leavened bread shall be seen among you, nor shall leaven be seen among you in all your quarters" (NKJV).

Before the Feasts of Passover and Unleavened Bread could be celebrated, all the leaven was to be removed from the Hebrew's house. This required a great amount of spring housecleaning. Everything in the house was thoroughly washed, scrubbed and cleaned. This included the walls, ceilings, floors, furniture, cabinets, etc. The cookingware was boiled in water and special utensils were used that had not been contaminated with leaven.

Once the cleaning was complete, the family would participate in a ceremony called the "search for the leaven." After dark, the head of the house would take a lighted candle and diligently search through every nook and cranny of the house looking for any hidden leaven. If he found any, he would immediately remove it from the house.

Many modern Hebrew families participate in this same housecleaning and search for the leaven. Just before Passover, crumbs of leavened bread are placed in each room of the house by one member of the family. Then the master of the house proceeds from room to room looking for the hidden leaven. The family member goes along carrying a lighted candle to expose where the leaven is hidden. When the head of the house finds the leaven, he is very careful not to touch it. To avoid contact, he takes a feather and brushes the leaven into a small wooden spoon. After he finds all the leaven, he puts the wooden spoon, the feather, and candle in a cloth bound by string, and burns it all. With the leaven now purged from the household, the Hebrew family is ready to celebrate the Feasts of Passover and Unleavened Bread.

We see in this feast, that its purpose was to remind the Hebrews that God had called them out of Egypt to be a separate people unto Himself. It was a permanent reminder that they had been delivered from Egypt and were to put off the philosophies and ways of Egypt and the bondage, oppression, sorrow, and suffering that was part of their old life.

How Jesus fulfilled

Jesus fulfilled the feast as the bread of life from heaven who had no leaven (sin) in Him. Because of the fermenting and permeating nature of leaven, it is commonly used as a metaphor for sin. There was no leaven of sin in Jesus Christ (2 Corinthians 5:21; 1 John 3:5).

Jesus pointed to Himself as the fulfillment of this feast the very same week it was being celebrated in Jerusalem. Many Jews had come to Jerusalem to celebrate the feast according to God's command (Exodus 23:14-17; Deuteronomy 16:16). A huge crowd of these pilgrims had heard about Jesus and were following Him wherever He went. But a problem developed. The crowd was hungry and there was nothing to eat. Jesus took this opportunity to perform a miracle that would point the people to Himself as the true bread of life.

Here's what happened. Jesus tested Philip, His disciple, by asking him how they would feed all the hungry people. Philip had no solution. Then another disciple, Andrew, brought a young boy to Jesus who had fives loaves of barley and two fish. But this obviously was inadequate. Yet Jesus took the boy's lunch, blessed it, and multiplied it so that there was enough to feed 5,000 men, plus women and children, and have some left over.

With this miracle fresh on their mind, Jesus spoke to the crowd the next morning about their need to come to Him as the bread of God who could give them eternal life. John was an eyewitness and gives us the following account: "Then Jesus said to them, 'Most assuredly I say to you, Moses did not give you the bread from heaven, but My Father gives you the true bread from heaven. For the bread of God is He who comes down from heaven and gives life to the world.' Then they said to Him, 'Lord, give us this bread always.' And Jesus said to them, 'I am the bread of life. He who comes to Me shall never hunger, and he who believes in me shall never thirst' " (John 6:32-35, NKJV).

After Jesus made these statements about Himself, the people murmured against Him. But Jesus would not back down from His claim to be the unleavened bread of God in the flesh. He repeated Himself to drive home His point, saying again, " 'Most assuredly, I say to you, he who believes in Me has everlasting life. I am the bread of life. Your fathers ate the manna in the wilderness, and are dead. I am the living bread which came down from heaven. If anyone eats of this bread, he will live forever; and the bread that I shall give is My flesh, which I shall give for the life of the world' " (John 6:47-51, NKJV).

Once more the people murmured and argued among themselves over Jesus' sayings. Jesus pressed His point a third time with these words, " 'Most assuredly, I say to you, unless you eat the flesh of the Son of Man and drink His blood, you have no life in you. Whoever eats My flesh and drinks My blood has eternal life, and I will raise him up at the last day. For My flesh is food indeed, and My blood is drink indeed. He who eats My flesh and drinks My blood abides in Me, and I in him. As the living Father sent Me, and I live because of the Father, so he who feeds on Me will live because of Me. This is the bread which came down from heaven—not as your fathers ate the manna, and are dead. He who eats the bread will live forever' " (John 6:53-58, NKJV).

In the previous chapter, we learned that Jesus was crucified on the fourteenth, a Thursday. We also noted that His body was taken down from the cross before six o'clock that evening which would begin the start of the next day. From this, we learn that Joseph of Arimathea and Nicodemus prepared Jesus' body for burial and placed Him in Joseph's tomb just in time for Jesus to be buried on the fifteenth which was the first day of the Feast of Unleavened Bread.

Jesus, as the unleavened bread from heaven, took on all of our leaven of sin and was buried on the same day the Jews had been celebrating the feast for 1,500 years. What the Jews had been portraying in the Feast of Unleavened Bread was a visual aid pointing them to Messiah Jesus who had come and fulfilled in His flesh the reality pictured by the feast.

Jesus took our leaven of sin with Him into the grave in His body, and into hell in His soul and spirit. There, for three days and three nights during the Feast of Unleavened Bread, Jesus paid the full penalty for our sins. He who knew no leaven (sin) became leaven (sin) for us. Our worldly attitudes and sinful ways were buried with Him. The bondage, oppression, sorrow, and suffering that was part of our old life went with Him into the grave. This is how Jesus fulfilled the Feast of Unleavened Bread.

Personal application

As believers in the Lord Jesus Christ, we are to put off the old leaven of sin that was crucified and buried with Him.

Paul wrote, "Put off your old nature which belongs to your former manner of life and is corrupt through deceitful lusts" (Ephesians 4:22, RSV).

The old nature or old man which Paul is speaking of is the sin nature that is within each of us. This old man within us naturally loves to sin. As long as it is the ruling force in our life we will commit outward acts of specific sins.

Jesus said it this way, "For from within, out of men's hearts, come evil thoughts of lust, theft, murder, adultery, wanting what belongs to others, wickedness, deceit, lewdness, envy, slander, pride, and all other folly. All these vile things come from within; they are what pollute you and make you unfit for God" (Mark 7:21-23, TLB).

The phrase "put off" which Paul used refers to a person taking off his garment. In Bible times, a person's garment could represent the person. We learn from this that Paul is saying we should out off the old sinful nature or old man that he describes in Galatians 5 as the works of the flesh. Paul writes, "Now the works of the flesh are evident, which are: adultery, fornication, uncleanness, licentiousness, idolatry, sorcery, hatred, contentions, jealousies, outbursts of wrath, selfish ambitions, dissensions, heresies, envy, murders, drunkenness, revelries, and the like; of which I tell you beforehand, just as I also told you in time past, that those who practice such things will not inherit the kingdom of God" (Galatians 5:19-21, NKJV).

We are able to put off this old man for He was buried with Christ in fulfillment of the Feast of Unleavened Bread. In this way, the power of sin over us has been broken. When we realize and appropriate this particular work of Christ on our behalf, God begins to work changes in our life. This is how the Feast of Unleavened Bread as realized in Jesus affects our condition.

God gave the Feast of Unleavened Bread as a means of showing the Hebrews they were to be separate from Egypt. In the Bible, Egypt represents the world system. The world system in which we live is evil. Its philosophies and ways are contrary to the Word of God. The Hebrews were to live differently once they were delivered from Egypt. Likewise, we who have been delivered from the world system through the blood of Jesus Christ are also to live a life separated from the attitudes and ways of the world.

God has chosen us who are believers in the Lord Jesus Christ to be a people set apart and different from those around us. We are to be in the world, but not of the world. This is the biblical meaning of the word "holy."

Paul expressed it this way to the Romans, "I beseech you therefore, brethren, by the mercies of God, that you present your bodies a living sacrifice, holy, acceptable to God, which is your reasonable service. And do not be conformed to this world, but be transformed by the renewing of your mind, that you may prove what is that good and acceptable and perfect will of God" (Romans 12:1-2, NKJV).

John wrote, "Do not love the world or the things in the world. If anyone loves the world, the love of the Father is not in him. For all that is in the world—the lust of the flesh, the lust of the eyes, and the pride of life—is not of the Father but is of the world. And the world is passing away, and the lust of it; but he who does the will of God abides forever" (1 John 2:15-17, NKJV).

Peter said, "Beloved, I beg you as sojourners and pilgrims, abstain from fleshly lusts which war against the soul" (1 Peter 2:11, NKJV).

Paul instructed the Corinthians, "Therefore come out from among them and be separate, says the Lord" (2 Corinthians 6:17, NKJV).

The Feasts of Unleavened Bread and First Fruits

represent the work of God in us that enables us to live this holy or separate life. The Bible calls this transforming work of God "sanctification" (see 1 Thessalonians 4:3-4; 2 Thessalonians 2:13; 1 Peter 1:2). This is a cooperative walk with God whereby we allow Him to conform us into the moral image of Jesus Christ (2 Corinthians 3:18).

This is what Paul had in mind when he wrote, ". . . work out your own salvation with fear and trembling; for it is God who works in you both to will and to do for His good pleasure" (Philippians 2:12-13, NKJV).

The Feast of Passover is the first step in our walk with God. It relates to our position of justification. The Feast of Unleavened Bread and First Fruits symbolize our next two steps. They relate to our condition of sanctification. The Feast of Unleavened Bread teaches us to put off the old man by appropriating the finished work of Jesus Christ as the true bread of God who took our sins with Him in the grave.

Seasonal aspect

You will notice from the chart that both the Feast of Unleavened Bread and First Fruits are connected with the Wesleys. God raised up Martin Luther in the 1500s for the purpose of restoring the spiritual significance of the Feast of Passover to the Church. This relates to our position before God. Our position before God must be right before our condition can be right. Since this is the beginning step in our spiritual journey, God restored it to the Church first.

God then used the Wesleys 200 years later to restore to the Church the spiritual significance of the Feasts of Unleavened Bread and First Fruits. God would use the Wesleys to show us that there's more to being a Christian than just having our sins forgiven.

John and Charles Wesley were born in England to devoutly religious parents. John was born in 1703 and

Charles came along four years later. Both attended Oxford University where Charles started the Holy Club. The Holy Club was a small gathering of like-minded men who desired to live a disciplined life for the purpose of developing inward holiness. The members committed themselves to regular private devotions and met each evening for Bible study and prayer.

John soon became the leader of the Holy Club. As he meditated on God's Word, he began to see that "true religion was seated in the heart, and that God's law extended to all our thoughts, as well as to words and actions." In other words, John saw that God was not only interested in our position, but that He also was interested in our condition.

This insight became a spiritual reality in John Wesley's own life on May 24, 1738 while he was attending a Christian gathering on Aldersgate Street in London. As the preacher was reading Martin Luther's comments on Paul's letter to the Romans, John felt his heart "strangely warmed" by the Spirit of God. Charles had a similar experience three days earlier.

This personal encounter with the living Lord totally transformed the Wesleys. The Holy Spirit became the dynamic force of their life, and their preaching focused on the necessity for personal holiness in the lives of those who professed Christ as Lord and Savior.

Chapter Three
Review Exercise

1. Describe how Jesus fulfilled the Feast of Unleavened Bread.

2. How does the Feast of Unleavened Bread as revealed through Jesus apply to our lives today?

3. Describe the seasonal aspect of the Feast of Unleavened Bread.

4
First Fruits

The third step in our walk with God is represented by the Feast of First Fruits. As with the Feast of Unleavened Bread, it too relates to our condition as believers in the Lord Jesus Christ. These feasts show the two different phases of Christian commitment that are necessary to change our spiritual condition, which are separation and consecration. Whereas the Feast of Unleavened Bread teaches about separation, the Feast of First Fruits teaches us about consecration.

Historical background

God gives the following instructions concerning this feast: "And the Lord spoke to Moses, saying, 'Speak to the children of Israel, and say to them: When you come into the land which I give to you, and reap its harvest, then you shall bring a sheaf of the first fruits of your harvest to the priest. He shall wave the sheaf before the LORD, to be accepted on your behalf; on the day after the Sabbath the priest shall wave it. And you shall offer on that day, when you wave the sheaf, a male lamb of the first year, without blemish, as a burnt offering to the LORD. Its grain offering shall be two-tenths of an ephah of fine flour mixed with oil, an offering made by fire to the LORD, for a sweet aroma; and its drink offering shall be of wine, one-fourth of a hin. You shall eat neither bread nor parched grain nor fresh grain until the same day that you have brought an offering to your God; it shall be a statute forever throughout your generation in all your dwelling' " (Leviticus 23:9-14, NKJV).

We learn in verse eleven that the Feast of First Fruits was to be celebrated on the day after the Sabbath. The Sabbath that is spoken of here is the regular Saturday Sabbath. This means that the Feast of First Fruits came on a Sunday. Notice on the chart that this was the seventeenth day of the month which was during the Feast of Unleavened Bread.

The Hebrews were to bring the first sheaves of the barley harvest and wave them before the Lord. At the beginning of the day, representative leaders of the people would cut certain barley sheaves that had been set apart just for this purpose and bring them to the priest. The priest would then present them to the Lord by waving them back and forth.

The purpose of this was to consecrate the harvest to God. The first fruits was representative of the whole harvest. This act reminded the Hebrews that God had given them the land and that all of the harvest rightfully belonged to Him. The people were just stewards of the land and so offering the first fruits actually consecrated the entire harvest to God.

How Jesus fulfilled

Jesus fulfilled this feast when He was resurrected as the first fruits from the dead. His resurrection marked the beginning of the harvest of souls who have been set apart for God through the Lord Jesus Christ.

Paul spoke of Jesus as the fulfillment of this feast with these words, "But now Christ is risen from the dead, and has become the firstfruits of those who have fallen asleep. For since by man came death, by Man also came the resurrection of the dead. For as in Adam all die, even so in Christ all shall be made alive. But each one in his own order: Christ the first fruits, afterward those who are Christ's at His coming" (1 Corinthians 15:20-23, NKJV).

Jesus was that human sheaf that God has set apart for the purpose of conquering death and providing eternal life for all who would acknowledge Him as Lord and Savior. As such, He was the first to rise from the dead who would never die again.

In fulfulling the Feast of Passover, Jesus was crucified on Thursday, the fourteenth. To fulfill the Feast of Unleavened Bread, He was buried on Friday, the fifteenth. The word Sabbath means rest. Jesus' body rested in the tomb on this day. Then on Sunday the seventeenth, Jesus rose from the dead in fulfullment of the Feast of First Fruits.

Matthew gives us this record of Jesus' resurrection: "Now after the Sabbath, as the first day of the week began to dawn, Mary Magdalene and the other Mary came to see the tomb. And behold, there was a great earthquake; for an angel of the Lord descended from heaven, and came and rolled back the stone from the door, and sat on it. His countenance was like lightning, and his clothing as white as snow. And the guards shook for fear of him, and became like dead men. But the angel answered and said to the women, 'Do not be afraid, for I know that you seek Jesus who was crucified. He is not here; for He is risen, as He said. Come, see the place where the Lord lay' " (Matthew 28:1-6, NKJV).

John added some further details and mentions the following statement by Jesus to Mary, "Touch me not, for I am not yet ascended to my Father; but go to my brethren, and say unto them, I ascend unto my Father, and your Father; and to my God, and your God" (John 20:17, KJV).

Jesus was going to ascend to the Father for the purpose of presenting Himself as the first fruits from the dead. He is our great High Priest who offered Himself in fulfillment of the Feast of First Fruits on the exact same day that the barley sheaves were being waved before the Lord.

The barley sheaf which was waved before the Lord consisted of a number of individual barley stalks that had been bundled together. Likewise, when Jesus offered Himself as the first fruits from the dead, many individual believers were raised with Him. Matthew writes, "and the graves were opened; and many bodies of the saints who had fallen asleep were raised; and coming out of the graves after His resurrection, they went into the holy city and appeared to many" (Matthew 27:52-53, NKJV).

When the time came to harvest the crop, the farmer would go into his field and inspect the first fruits of the crop. If he accepted the first fruits, then the rest of the harvest would also be acceptable to him. God our heavenly Father has accepted Jesus as the first fruits from the dead. Therefore, you too are acceptable to God, and He will also raise you from the dead if you have a personal relationship with Jesus Christ as your Lord and Savior.

Paul expressed this truth to the Christians in Rome by these words, "But if the Spirit of Him who raised Jesus from the dead dwells in you, He who raised Christ from the dead will also give life to your mortal bodies through His Spirit who dwells in you" (Romans 8:11, NKJV).

Jesus, as the first fruits, is our representative. By presenting Himself, He consecrated the rest of us to the Father. As Paul so clearly and boldly said to the Ephesian Christians, "He [God] has made us accepted in the Beloved" (Ephesians 1:6, NKJV). We believers are the human stalks that have been bundled together with Christ. Therefore, "if the firstfruit is holy, the lump is also holy; and if the root is holy, so are the branches" (Romans 11:16, NKJV).

First Corinthians 15:51-57 reads, "Behold, I tell you a mystery: We shall not all sleep, but we shall all be changed—

in a moment, in the twinkling of an eye, at the last trumpet. For the trumpet will sound, and the dead will be raised incorruptible, and we shall be changed. For this corruptible must put on incorruption, and this mortal must put on immortality. So when this corruptible has put on incorruption, and this mortal has put on immortality, then shall be brought to pass the saying that is written: 'Death is swallowed up in victory. O Death, where is your sting? O Hades, where is your victory?' The sting of death is sin, and the strength of sin is the law. But thanks be to God, who gives us the victory through our Lord Jesus Christ. Therefore, my beloved brethren, be steadfast, immovable, always abounding in the work of the Lord, knowing that your labor is not in vain in the Lord" (NKJV).

We also learn in Paul's letter to the Thessalonian Christians, "But I do not want you to be ignorant, brethren, concerning those who have fallen asleep, lest you sorrow as others who have no hope. For if we believe that Jesus died and rose again, even so God will bring with Him those who sleep in Jesus. For this we say to you by the word of the Lord, that we who are alive and remain until the coming of the Lord will by no means precede those who are asleep. For the Lord Himself will descend from heaven with a shout, with the voice of an archangel, and with the trumpet of God. And the dead in Christ will rise first. Then we who are alive and remain shall be caught up together with them in the clouds to meet the Lord in the air. And thus we shall always be with the Lord" (1 Thessalonians 4:13-17, NKJV). "For God did not appoint us to wrath, but to obtain salvation through our Lord Jesus Christ, who died for us, that whether we wake or sleep, we should live together with Him. Therefore comfort each other and edify one another, just as you also are doing" (1 Thessalonians 5:9-11, NKJV).

When Lazarus died, his sister came to Jesus for comfort. John records the following conversation: "Then Martha, as soon as she heard that Jesus was coming, went and met Him, but Mary was sitting in the house. Then Martha said to Jesus, 'Lord, if You had been here, my brother would not have died. But even now I know that whatever You ask of God, God will give You.' Jesus said to her, 'Your brother will rise again.' Martha said to Him, 'I know that he will rise again in the resurrection at the last day.' Jesus said to her, 'I am the resurrection and the life. He who believes in Me, though he may die, he shall live. And whoever lives and believes in Me shall never die. Do you believe this?' " (John 11:21-26. NKJV).

Job expressed this hope for believers of all ages when he said, "For I know that my redeemer liveth, and that he shall stand at the latter day upon the earth: And though after my skin worms destroy this body, yet in my flesh shall I see God" (Job 19:25-26, KJV).

Personal application

The Feasts of Unleavened Bread and First Fruits represent two phases of Christian commitment which are necessary to change our spiritual condition. Unleavened Bread teaches about being buried with Christ, which indicates we should live a life separated from the attitudes and ways of the world. This involves our putting off the old man of sin, characterized by the works of the flesh.

The Feast of First Fruits teaches us about our resurrection with Christ in our spirit as well as our future bodily resurrection. We are saved from our old life to live in the resurrected life of Jesus Christ today. Putting off the old man is not enough. We must also put on the new man. After Paul told the Ephesian Christians to put off the old man, he then said, "and put on the new nature, created after the likeness of God in true righteousness and holiness" (Ephesians 4:24, RSV). This new nature Paul is speaking of is the very nature of God coming within us through the person of the Holy Spirit.

We put on this new man by allowing the Holy Spirit to live the resurrected life of Jesus Christ through us. Paul had this exchange of natures in mind when he wrote to the Corinthians, "Therefore if any man be in Christ, he is a new creature: old things are passed away, behold all things are become new" (2 Corinthians 5:17, KJV). We who were dead in our trespasses and sins have been raised up with Christ in our spirit-man to walk in newness of life.

Paul summarized this with these words, "I have been crucified with Christ; it is no longer I who live, but Christ who lives in me; and the life I now live in the flesh I live by faith in the Son of God, who loved me and gave himself for me" (Galatians 2:20, RSV).

Paul expressed this to the Christians in Rome in the following way, "Likewise you also, reckon yourselves to be dead indeed to sin, but alive to God in Christ Jesus our Lord. Therefore do not let sin reign in your mortal body, that you should obey it in its lusts. And do not present your members as instruments of unrighteousness to sin, but present yourselves to God as being alive from the dead, and your members as instruments of righteousness to God. For sin shall not have dominion over you, for you are not under law but under grace" (Romans 6:11-14, NKJV).

The new man, then, is simply Christ living in us through the person of the Holy Spirit. Paul wrote to the Galatians, "I say then: Walk in the Spirit; and you shall not fulfill the lust of the flesh" (Galatians 5:16, NKJV).

When we walk in the Spirit, the character of Jesus Christ will be the dominant force in our life. Paul refers to the character of Christ as the fruit of the Spirit and describes it with these words, "But the fruit of the Spirit is love, joy, peace, longsuffering, kindness, goodness, faithfulness, gentleness, self-control" (Galatians 5:22-23, NKJV).

When we live in the character of Jesus Christ, we not only have peace with God but we also enjoy the peace of God (Colossians 3:15). Many Christians do not experience this divine blessing because they have never separated themselves from the things of the world and consecrated themselves to the lordship of Jesus Christ.

James wrote that we who have put our trust in Christ and have received His Spirit are a kind of first fruits of God's creatures (James 1:18). By this, James meant that we are the first of all of God's creation to experience the new life that God has decreed for planet earth and its inhabitants through the redeeming work of Jesus Christ. In view of this, we present ourselves as a living wave offering to God, and by doing so, acknowledge that we belong to Him.

Seasonal aspect

As mentioned in the previous chapter and noted on the chart, the spiritual significance of both the Feasts of Unleavened Bread and First Fruits were restored to the Church during the 1700s primarily through the ministry of John and Charles Wesley.

John and Charles complemented each other in their ministry in a unique manner. Whereas John was a powerful preacher, Charles was a prolific songwriter. In the course of their ministry, John traveled over 250,000 miles preaching the gospel, mostly on horseback, and Charles penned over 7,000 Christian songs and poems. In this way the people not only heard the Word of God, they also learned to sing it. In many respects, Charles' songs had as much effect on the listeners as John's sermons.

Because their ministry was not received by the institutional church (same as with Luther), the Wesleys were forced to take their message to the toiling masses of working class people who had been ignored by the Church of England. Although they met considerable opposition, the grace and power of God worked through them in a most unusual way to breathe fresh life into the Church.

God used the Wesleys to radically change the society and social ills of their day. By emphasizing personal holiness and a change in one's condition as well as their position, the Wesleys initiated a lasting spiritual renewal that restored Christian salt and light to a decaying and darkened world.

Chapter Four
Review Exercise

1. Describe how Jesus fulfilled the Feast of First Fruits.

2. How does the Feast of First Fruits through Jesus apply to our lives today?

3. Describe the seasonal aspect of the Feast of First Fruits.

5
pentecost

The three feasts seasons of Passover, Pentecost, and Tabernacles represent three major encounters God has with His covenant people. The feast season known as Passover was established by God for the purpose of teaching us how to find God's peace. We find peace with God when we appropriate Jesus as the Passover Lamb who died for our sins. We find the peace of God through Jesus as our Unleavened Bread and First Fruits representative. This work of Jesus on our behalf is realized personally when we set ourselves apart from the ways of the world and give ourselves completely to Jesus as Lord and master. The result is that we not only have peace with God, but we also enjoy the peace of God.

This is certainly a great blessing that God has provided for us. But that's not all God has for us. He not only desires that we know His peace, but that we also know His power. He has made His power available to us through Jesus Christ. By using the Feast of Pentecost as a visual aid, God teaches us how to receive this power. Thus, the Feast of Pentecost represents the second major encounter the Christian can have with God. Taken in order of the feasts, it is the fourth step the believer must take towards the rest of God.

Historical background

God gives the following instructions concerning the Feast of Pentecost, "And you shall count for yourselves from the day after the Sabbath, from the day that you brought the sheaf of the wave offering: seven Sabbaths shall be completed. Count fifty days to the day after the seventh Sabbath; then you shall offer a new grain offering to the LORD. You shall bring from your habitations two wave loaves of two-tenths of an ephah. They shall be of fine flour; they shall be baked with leaven. They are the firstfruits to the LORD. And you shall offer with the bread seven lambs of the first year, without blemish, one young bull, and two rams. They shall be as a burnt offering to the LORD, with their grain offering and their drink offerings, an offering made by fire for a sweet aroma to the LORD. Then you shall sacrifice one kid of the goats as a sin offering, and two male lambs of the first year as a sacrifice of peace offering. The priest shall wave them with the bread of the firstfruits as a wave offering before the LORD, with the two lambs. They shall be holy to the LORD for the priest. And you shall proclaim on the same day that it is a holy convocation to you. You shall do no customary work on it. It shall be a statute forever in all your dwellings throughout your generations" (Leviticus 23:15-21, NKJV).

The Feast of Passover, you recall, marked the beginning of the barley harvest while the Feast of Pentecost was celebrated at the completion of the wheat harvest. Notice from the chart that it came on the sixth day of the Hebrew month of Sivan. This corresponds to our months of May and June. It lasted for one day.

The instructions God gave in verses fifteen and sixteen enable us to determine this exact date of the feast. God said they were to celebrate the feast fifty days after the Feast of First Fruits. As we've learned, the Feast of First Fruits was celebrated on the seventeenth of Nisan. Fifty days later falls on the sixth of Sivan. Since the word Pentecost in Greek means fifty, this feast gets it name from the fifty day interval between the two dates. The Feast of Pentecost also was referred to as the Feast of Weeks, Feast of Harvest, and Day of First Fruits (Exodus 23:16; 34:22; Numbers 28:26).

The main activity on the Feast of Pentecost was the presentation of a wave offering to the Lord, two loaves of bread baked with leaven. This bread was made of fine flour that had been carefully sifted to separate the coarse matter from the wheat. The wave offering expressed the Hebrews' dependence on God for the harvest and their daily bread. So this was a thanksgiving offering.

Later when the Jews were dispersed among the nations, the Feast of Pentecost lost its primary significance as a harvest festival and was celebrated as a memorial to the time when God gave them the law at Mount Sinai.

By careful calculation of time, the Jews have traditionally believed that God gave the law to Moses on the day of Pentecost. We learn in Exodus 19 that the Jews arrived at the Sinai in the third month on the Hebrew calendar and possibly on the third day (Exodus 19:1). Looking back at the Jewish calendar in Chapter Two, we see that Sivan is the third month on the sacred calendar. Three days later, on the sixth of Sivan, God came down upon Mount Sinai and gave them the law (Exodus 19:11).

How Jesus fulfilled

Jesus fulfilled the Feast of Pentecost as He was glorified and exalted to the throne of God from which He sent the Holy Spirit upon His disciples on the Day of Pentecost.

Jesus spoke of Himself as the fulfillment of this feast with these words, ". . . The hour has come that the Son of Man should be glorified. Most assuredly, I say to you, unless a grain of wheat falls into the ground and dies, it remains alone; but if it dies, it produces much grain" (John 12:23-24, NKJV).

Jesus was talking about Himself as the human grain of wheat who would die for the sins of the world. In the Bible, fine flour represents perfect righteousness. Jesus was perfectly righteous. There was no coarse matter (sin) in Him. Yet, as the wheat was crushed, sifted, and baked in order to become bread, so Jesus was crushed, sifted, and baked in the ovens of hell for our sins. But because Jesus had never sinned, death and hell could not hold Him (Revelation 1:18). In view of this, He was resurrected as the first fruits from the dead.

As we've just learned, it was fifty days from the Feast of First Fruits to the Feast of Pentecost. Likewise, it was exactly fifty days from Jesus' resurrection to the day when He sent the Holy Spirit upon His disciples (note chart).

The Day of Pentecost did not originate with Christianity, but it is the Jewish feast day that God chose to send the Holy Spirit as proof that Jesus had been glorified as Lord. This was a day when the Hebrews would be in Jerusalem to celebrate the feast and the giving of the law.

On the evening that Jesus was resurrected (the seventeenth) He appeared to His disciples and breathed eternal life into them. John recorded this event and wrote, "Then the same day at evening, being the first day of the week, when the doors were shut where the disciples were assembled, for fear of the Jews, Jesus came and stood in the midst, and said to them, 'Peace be with you.' Now when He had said this, He showed them His hands and His side. Then the disciples were glad when they saw the Lord. Then Jesus said to them again, 'Peace to you! As the Father has sent Me, I also send you.' And when He had said this,

He breathed on them, and said to them, 'Receive the Holy Spirit' " (John 20:19-22, NKJV).

We see at this occasion that Jesus gave the Holy Spirit to the disciples. This was their spiritual rebirth which established their new life position as believers in the Lord Jesus Christ. If they had all died that night, they would have gone to heaven. In other words, they were "saved."

But Jesus had something better planned for them. He wanted to bring heaven down to them. But it was not yet time to do so. Therefore, He spent the next forty days with the disciples explaining how all the Old Testament pointed to Him. Then when the time came for Jesus to ascend back to heaven, He told the disciples to wait in Jerusalem until He would send the promise of the Father, at which time they would be filled with the Holy Spirit for power.

Luke writes this for us, "Then He said to them, 'These are the words which I spoke to you while I was still with you, that all things must be fulfilled which were written in the Law of Moses and the Prophets and the Psalms concerning Me.' And He opened their understanding, that they might comprehend the Scriptures. Then He said to them, 'Thus it is written, and thus it was necessary for the Christ to suffer and to rise from the dead on the third day, and that repentance and remission of sins should be preached in His name to all nations, beginning at Jerusalem. And you are witnesses of these things. Behold, I send the Promise of My Father upon you; but tarry in the city of Jerusalem until you are endued with power from on high.' And He led them out as far as Bethany, and He lifted up His hands and blessed them. Now it came to pass, while He blessed them, that He was parted from them and carried up into heaven. And they worshiped Him, and returned to Jerusalem with great joy, and were continually in the temple praising and blessing God. Amen." (Luke 24:44-53, NKJV).

Later, in the book of Acts, Luke recalls the conversation Jesus had with the disciples. He writes, "And being assembled together with them, He commanded them not to depart from Jerusalem, but to wait for the Promise of the Father, which, He said, 'you have heard from Me; for John truly baptized with water, but you shall be baptized with the Holy Spirit not many days from now.' Therefore, when they had come together, they asked Him, saying, 'Lord will You at this time restore the kingdom to Israel?' And He said to them, 'It is not for you to know times or seasons which the Father has put in His own authority. But you shall receive power when the Holy Spirit has come upon you; and you shall be witnesses to Me in Jerusalem, and in all Judea and Samaria, and to the end of the earth' " (Acts 1:4-8, NKJV).

Luke reviews the words of Jesus instructing His disciples to wait in Jerusalem until they receive the Promise of the Father. According to Luke, Jesus equates the Promise of the Father with the baptism in the Holy Spirit. He says the purpose of the baptism in the Holy Spirit is to give the disciples power to be witnesses to Jesus. They would have this encounter ten days later on the day of Pentecost.

About 120 of Jesus' followers then gathered in an upper room waiting in prayer for this blessed event. Luke records what happened on that glorious day. He wrote, "Now when the Day of Pentecost had fully come, they were all with one accord in one place. And suddenly there came a sound from heaven, as of a rushing mighty wind, and it filled the whole house where they were sitting. Then there appeared to them divided tongues, as of fire, and one sat upon each of them. And they were all filled with the Holy Spirit and began to speak with other tongues, as the Spirit gave them utterance. Now there were dwelling in Jerusalem Jews, devout men, from every nation under heaven. And when this sound occurred, the multitude came together, and were confused, because everyone heard them speak in his own language. Then they were all amazed and marveled, saying to one another, 'Look, are not all these who speak Galileans? And how is it that we hear, each in our own language in which we were born' " (Acts 2:1-8, NKJV)?

From Luke's account, we see the marvelous timing of God. Thousands of Jews had journeyed to Jerusalem to celebrate the Feast of Pentecost. This feast symbolized their second major encounter with God. But it was only symbolic. It is true that God gave them the law on this day. But the law could not provide them with power. The law was not the Promise of the Father. The reality which the Feast of Pentecost had visualized for centuries was the anointing of the disciples with spiritual power for the purpose of enabling them to be effective witnesses to the lordship of Jesus Christ.

According to Luke's record, when the disciples were filled with the Holy Spirit, they began to worship God in the foreign languages that were spoken and understood by the Jewish pilgrims who had journeyed to Jerusalem to keep the feast. These were languages that the disciples themselves did not know. There was such a loud noise accompanying this experience that it attracted the attention of the Jewish visitors who went to see what the commotion was all about.

As they approached the place where the noise was coming from, they heard the disciples worshiping God in the various languages represented by the Jews' homeland. Peter then stood up and preached a bold sermon to this Jewish crowd in their common language of either Aramaic or Greek. About three thousand responded to Peter's sermon by accepting Jesus as their Messiah and Lord.

This outpouring of the Holy Spirit was taking place on the very day that the Jews were offering the two wave loaves to God symbolizing their dependence on Him. Remember that the loaves were baked with leaven (a common symbol of sin). One of these leavened loaves was pointing to the Jews, who although they were sinners, would receive the power of God in their lives as they acknowledged Jesus as Lord (the fine flour). This happened on the exact day the Jews had been celebrating the Feast of Pentecost for almost 1,500 years.

But what about the other loaf? The other loaf represented the Gentiles who would also receive this blessing from God even though, they too, were sinners. When Peter preached his sermon to the Jews, he said the Promise of the Father (baptism in the Holy Spirit) was for everyone who would acknowledge Jesus as their Lord (see Acts 2:39).

There was a Gentile by the name of Cornelius who was seeking God with all his heart. An angel spoke to him in a vision instructing him to send for Peter who would come and preach to him and his friends. We read the following account of what happened: "While Peter was still speaking these words, the Holy Spirit fell upon all those who heard the word. And those of the circumcision who believed were astonished, as many as came with Peter, because the gift of the Holy Spirit had been poured out on the Gentiles also. For they heard them speak with tongues and magnify God. Then Peter answered, 'Can anyone forbid water, that these should not be baptized who have received the Holy Spirit just as we have?' "(Acts 10:44-47, NKJV).

Later, when Peter shared what happened at that meeting with his fellow Jewish believers, he said, "And as I began to speak, the Holy Spirit fell upon them, as upon us at the beginning. Then I remembered the word of the Lord, how He said, 'John indeed baptized with water, but you shall be baptized with the Holy Spirit' " (Acts 11:15-16, NKJV).

Now we see the significance of the fine flour and the two wave loaves of leaven. The fine flour represented Jesus who was perfectly righteous and without sin. The two wave loaves represented the Jew and Gentiles. Both have the leaven of sin in their lives. But both can receive the power of God to help them overcome that sin and live as effective witnesses to the lordship of Jesus Christ.

Personal application

John the Baptism introduced Jesus as the Lamb of God who takes away the sin of the world and baptizes in the Holy Spirit (John 1:29, 33; Matthew 3:11; Mark 1:8; Luke 3:16). Jesus fulfilled the Feast of Passover as the Lamb of God who died on the cross for our sins. He fulfilled the Feast of Pentecost as the exalted and glorified Lord who baptizes in the Holy Spirit.

Passover represents the first major encounter with God by His covenant people. Pentecost represents the second encounter. God wants us to know Jesus, not only as the crucified Lamb of God who died for our sins, but also as the living glorified Lord who baptizes us in the Holy Spirit.

If there was ever a group of people who should have been prepared to minister in the power of the Holy Spirit, it was the disciples. They didn't go to seminary; they had something better. They had Jesus as their teacher for over three years. In addition to His teachings, they watched Him perform many miracles. They saw Him conquer death and stand in their midst in a resurrected body. Jesus then gave them the Holy Spirit and they were born again. The Holy Spirit came to live in them for the purpose of giving them eternal life.

The purpose of the baptism in the Holy Spirit is to give us power so that we might be bold witnesses to the lordship of Jesus Christ (Acts 1:8). It was this second major encounter with God, not the resurrection, that transformed Peter from being a coward hiding behind closed doors to the man who stood before the great crowd and boldly proclaimed that Jesus is Lord.

Peter was a different man. He was no longer timid. He was no longer a closet Christian. Neither were the other disciples who were there with him. It wasn't the resurrection of Jesus that changed them, because even after Jesus appeared to them and gave them the indwelling Holy Spirit, He still told them to wait.

But, after they were filled with the Holy Spirit they began to minister in the Spirit. They began to minister in the power, boldness, and authority of Jesus Christ. This little band of ordinary men and women turned their world upside down after they received the baptism in the Holy Spirit. When they were born again at Passover, they received the Holy Spirit within for salvation. At Pentecost they were filled with the Holy Spirit for service.

Even Jesus had to be filled with the Holy Spirit before beginning His ministry. He had to have God's power in His life before He preached, healed the sick, cast out demons, and overcame Satan.

Jesus was filled with the Holy Spirit when He was baptized by John in the Jordan River. Matthew records the following account, "And Jesus, when He had been baptized, came up immediately from the water; and behold, the heavens were open to Him, and He saw the Spirit of God descending like a dove alighting upon Him. And suddenly a voice came from heaven saying, 'This is my beloved Son, in whom I am well pleased' " (Matthew 3:16-17, NKJV).

Jesus was now filled with the Holy Spirit. He was ready to begin His ministry. After a brief victorious encounter with Satan, Jesus went to Galilee. The Bible says He went in the power of the Spirit (Luke 4:14).

While in Galilee, Jesus visited His home town of Nazareth. He went to the synagogue and stood up to read the Scriptures. The book of Isaiah was given to Him and He began to read these words, "The Spirit of the Lord is upon Me, Because He has anointed Me to preach the gospel to the poor. He has sent Me to heal the brokenhearted, to preach deliverance to the captives and recovery of sight to the blind, to set at liberty those who are oppressed, to preach the acceptable year of the Lord" (Luke 4:18-19, NKJV).

This is the ministry of Jesus Christ. It also is the great commission Jesus has given to all Christians. He told His followers, "he who believes in Me, the works that I do he will do also, and greater works than these he will do, because I go to My Father" (John 14:12, NKJV).

Jesus said we would do greater works than He did because He was going to the Father. When Jesus went to the Father, He sent the Holy Spirit upon the disciples. When the Holy Spirit came upon the disciples, they received power to minister in the Spirit. They were the beginning of Jesus' promise that we would do greater works than He did.

When Jesus walked the earth, His ministry was limited to His human body. But now He ministers on earth through His spiritual body—the Church. But just as Jesus and the first disciples, we too must be filled with the Holy Spirit. God still wants us to use ordinary men and women to turn the world upside down as we minister in the Spirit.

Seasonal aspect

As the book of Acts reveals, the Church began in a blaze of glory. God worked through the early Christians in powerful ways.

Jesus gave these first believers the following commission and assurance: "And He said to them, 'Go into all the world and preach the gospel to every creature. He who believes and is baptized will be saved; but he who does not believe will be condemned. And these signs will follow those who believe: In My name they will cast out demons; they will speak with new tongues; they will take up serpents; and if they drink anything deadly, it will by no means hurt them; they will lay hands on the sick, and they will recover' " (Mark 16:15-18, NKJV).

Mark further writes, "So then, after the Lord had spoken to them, He was received up into heaven, and sat down at the right hand of God. And they went out and preached everywhere, the Lord working with them and confirming the word through the accompanying signs. Amen." (Mark 16:19-20, NKJV). This was a glorious beginning for the Church. But it didn't take long for man to begin to manipulate the moving of God.

Young Timothy was the elder of the church at Ephesus, and some of the people who were part of his congregation began to pressure him to quench the flow of the Holy Spirit. Word of this came to Paul, who was Timothy's spiritual father. In about A.D. 65, Paul wrote a letter to Timothy for the purpose of encouraging him to allow the Holy Spirit the freedom to manifest when the Church came together.

Paul instructed Timothy, "Do not neglect the gift that is in you, which was given to you by prophecy with the laying on of the hands of the presbytery" (1 Timothy 4:14, NKJV).

Timothy continued to allow these people to intimidate him so Paul wrote him a second time about three years later. He again spoke of this problem and said, "Therefore I remind you to stir up the gift of God which is in you through the laying on of my hands. For God has not given us a spirit of fear, but of power and of love and of a sound mind" (2 Timothy 1:6-7, NKJV).

When the church became institutionalized in A.D. 312, many of those in charge were politicians rather than religious leaders. Their decisions were more political than spiritual. The result was that Christianity was organized into a religious system whose leaders chose a human leadership rather than a spirit-directed leadership filled with the power of God.

God let man have his way because God will not force Himself on us. Unfortunately the spiritual reality of the Feast of Pentecost was lost to the Church, although there have always been periodic, localized revivals of Pentecostal power throughout church history.

You'll notice on the chart that God began to restore the power of Pentecost to the church on a worldwide basis in the early 1900s. There were two significant events.

The first took place on New Year's Day, 1901, at Bethel Bible College in Topeka, Kansas. Charles Parham was teaching on the baptism in the Holy Spirit, and encouraging the students to search the Scriptures regarding the subject. It was during this time of study that a Miss Agnes Ozman received the gift of speaking in tongues. Parham and several other students had a similar experience three days later.

This Pentecostal message, with its accompanying manifestations, soon spread to the surrounding states, and made its way into Texas, and finally out to California in 1906.

William Seymour arrived in Los Angeles to preach at a Nazarene Church but was not received because of his Pentecostal message. He then began to hold services in a converted livery stable at 312 Azusa Street. It was at this location that a mighty Pentecostal revival started which lasted for three years. This revival launched the modern worldwide Pentecostal movement. As news of the revival spread, many Christians from around the world came to the meetings at Azusa Street and took the message of Pentecost back with them to their homeland.

Because man is reluctant to hand over the leadership of the Church to the Holy Spirit, this restoration of the Feast of Pentecost was not received by the leaders of the mainline Christian denominations (same as with Luther and Wesley).

In the late 1950s and early 1960s, God again moved to restore the Feast of Pentecost to the Church in what has become known as the "charismatic renewal." This more recent revival of Pentecost has influenced all the historic Christian denominations, both Protestant and Catholic. The charismatic movement, though rejected by much of the institutional church, has spread throughout the world and become a major force in Christianity.

Chapter Five
Review Exercise

1. Describe how Jesus fulfilled the Feast of Pentecost.

2. How does the Feast of Pentecost through Jesus apply to our lives today?

3. Describe the seasonal aspect of the Feast of Pentecost.

6

tRumpets

The Feast of Tabernacles was the last of the required feast seasons. It included the Feasts of Trumpets, Atonement, and Tabernacles. As with Passover and Pentecost, all the Jewish males were required to journey to Jerualem for its celebration.

The Feast of Tabernacles was celebrated during the Hebrew month of Tishri (see chart). This was at the end of the harvest season. It is also was called the Feast of Ingathering (Exodus 23:16). By this time, all the harvest was complete and both the land and people were at rest.

The clear teaching of this feast season was that God wanted His covenant people to learn to rest in Him. Therefore, the Feast of Tabernacles represents the third major encounter the believer can have with God through the person and work of the Lord Jesus Christ.

The Feast of Passover teaches us about God's peace. The Feast of Pentecost teaches us about God's power. The Feast of Tabernacles teaches us about God's rest. God's rest is the place Christians come to in their walk with God where they find contentment in God just for who God is.

Before going further into the Feast of Tabernacles, it would be helpful for us to consider the period on the Hebrews calendar when there was no feast. These were the long summer months of Tammuz, Ab, and Elul.

As we've learned, the feasts were religious seasons representing God's dealings with the Jewish people as a nation. They symbolized major encounters between God and His covenant people. By the long summer months when there was no feast, God was very graphically showing the Jewish people that there would be a long period of time in the future when He would not make Himself known to them on a national basis. He would still be saving individual Jews, but His favor and attention would be directed towards the Gentiles. You see, God chose the Jews as the nation of people through which He would work out certain of His divine plans and purposes. God would use them to write down and preserve the Scriptures, to bring the Messiah into the world and proclaim the Gospel of Jesus Christ to all nations. The Jews fulfilled these first two callings but failed on the last because they rejected Jesus as their Messiah.

When the Jews rejected Jesus, God directed His attention towards the Gentiles. John said of Jesus, "He came to His own [Jews], and His own did not receive Him. But as many as received Him, to them [Gentiles] He gave the right to become children of God, even to those who believe in His name" (John 1:11-12, NKJV).

For the last 2,000 years God has given His favor and attention to the Gentiles. The Gentiles, not the Jews, have been greatly blessed by God. The Gentiles have had the encounters with God. The Gentiles have been the ones to spread the gospel of Jesus Christ. This span of time in history when God's attention is directed towards the Gentiles is referred to as the church period. It began with the Feast of Pentecost and will continue up to the future prophetic fulfillment of the Feast of Tabernacles. As noted on the chart, the three long summer months when there is no feast corresponds to the church period.

But because there still is another feast which will be literally fulfilled in the future, we understand that there will come a time when God will turn His attention back to the Jews and once again deal with them on a national basis. This third and final major encounter is the second coming of Jesus Christ. This is the prophetic significance of the Feast of Tabernacles. Because Israel has been restored as a nation, and the Jews once again occupy Jerusalem, we can know that God is even now dealing with the Jews as a nation. The church period is coming to a close and God is preparing the Jewish people for the return of Jesus Christ. This is what's happening in the world today. As we see Israel in the spotlight of world news, we can know that the return of Jesus Christ is near.

God amazingly revealed that this was His plan by strategically placing a comment about Gentiles in Leviticus 23. God stuck this comment right between the last verse of instruction on the Feast of Pentecost and the first verse of instruction on the Feast of Trumpets, which is part of the Feast of Tabernacles. I believe He did this purposefully as a sneak preview of what He had in mind all along.

Here is the comment to the Jews: "When you reap the harvest of your land, you shall not wholly reap the corners of your field when you reap, nor shall you gather any gleaning from your harvest. You shall leave them for the poor and the stranger: I am the LORD your God" (Leviticus 23:22, NKJV).

The key word for purposes of this discussion is the word stranger. It refers to Gentiles. The story of Ruth and Boaz was written in the Bible as an example of this particular instruction from God being obeyed. Boaz was a rich Jewish landowner. Ruth was a Gentile (Moabite) who gleaned in his fields. Ruth married Boaz and as a result became a partaker in the covenant promises God had made to Abraham. Likewise, the Gentiles have become partakers in in certain of the covenant promises to Abraham through their spiritual marriage to Jesus Christ. Boaz is a type or shadow of Christ, while Ruth is a type of the church. I think it's more than coincidence that God put this instruction where He did in the flow of discussion of the chapter.

The church period fills the great time gap between the two comings of Jesus Christ. He came the first time as the Passover Lamb who died for our sins. Then He sent the Holy Spirit to initiate the age of the church. When the church age is over, He will come a second time as the lion from the tribe of Judah to rule, not only as King of the Jews, but as King of kings and Lord of lords. The prophetic significance of the Feast of Tabernacles is that it represents the end of this age and the return of Jesus as God's final encounter with the Jewish people. Paul summarizes all of this in Romans 9-11.

As fascinating as this subject is, we must leave it now to learn about the Feast of Trumpets.

Historical background

God gave the following instructions in regard to the Feast of Trumpets, "Then the Lord spoke to Moses, saying, 'Speak to the children of Israel saying: "In the seventh month, on the first day of the month, you shall have a sabbath-rest, a memorial of blowing of trumpets, a holy convocation. You shall do no customary work on it; and you shall offer an offering made by fire to the Lord" ' " (Leviticus 23:23-25, NKJV).

We see from this Scripture reference and note on the chart that the Feast of Trumpets was on the first day of the seventh month on the religious calendar. This is the Hebrew month of Tishri which corresponds to the months of September and October on the Gentile calendar. Tishri is also the first month on the Jewish civil calendar and is the Jewish

New Year. The Hebrew name for this new year is Rosh Hashanah.

The main purpose of the Feast of Trumpets was to announce the arrival of the seventh month in order to prepare the people for the Day of Atonement which was ten days later. We'll discover the significance of this in the next chapter. The seventh month was special because it was the last month in the religious season. It was the time when God would complete His dealings with the people for that year. It also was the last time they were required to journey to Jerusalem until the following year at Passover.

The day was not marked by any special events other than the blowing of trumpets and the offering of sacrifices (Numbers 29:1-6). The Hebrews always blew trumpets on the first day of each month so everyone would know the new month had arrived (Numbers 10:10). But on the Feast of Trumpets they blew them extra long and extra loud, and they blew them all day. The type of trumpet blown was the ram's horn, for which the Hebrew word is *shofar*. The shofar was blown in remembrance of the ram that was sacrificed in place of Isaac (Genesis 22:13).

God used trumpets in the Old Testament as a means of communicating with His covenant people. God could not speak directly to the people without them being terrified. So He spoke to them indirectly through the use of trumpets.

To the Hebrews, the sound of the trumpet represented both the voice of God, and the might of God in warfare. A good summary of how the trumpets were used is provided in the tenth chapter of Numbers.

Originally, two silver trumpets were blown, but they were later replaced by the shofar. The silver trumpets were made from the same source of silver. They were blown to assemble the people to worship, to break camp in order to move on, and as an alarm in preparation for battle.

One of the clearest demonstrations of the use of trumpets in warfare is the story of Joshua at the battle of Jericho. Moses had died, and the leadership passed to Joshua who became responsible for leading the people into the promised land.

Joshua encountered one who identified himself as the commander of the army of the LORD (Joshua 5:13-15). This commander of God's army gave Joshua a strange battle plan. It is one that Joshua would never think of himself. And if he did, he certainly wouldn't tell anyone. They'd think he was crazy. But God doesn't do things the way man does.

The angel told Joshua to march his army around the city once each day for six days. Seven priests were to follow the army, each blowing a shofar. They were followed by another group of priests carrying the Ark of the Covenant, who were followed by a rear guard. All were to march in absolute silence. No one was to say a word. The only noise was the sound of the shofars blown by the priests.

On the seventh day, they were to march around the city seven times. Everyone was still to be quiet. Then at a certain point, Joshua was to give a command for the priests to blow one long, loud blast on the shofar. Then everyone was to shout! At that very moment, according to the commander of God's army, the walls of Jericho would fall down enabling the Hebrews to take the city (see Joshua 6).

Joshua carried out the battle plan given to him by the commander of God's army. It all happened just as God said and the Jews soundly defeated their enemy. As God spoke to the people and used trumpets to fight their battles for them, the Jews began to call God the "horn of their salvation." By this, they meant that God was their deliverer who would fight their battles for them and save them from their enemies.

King David was a great warrior who clearly understood and appreciated the might of God in warfare. He often spoke of God as the horn of his salvation. In Psalm 18, David says to God, "I will love you, O LORD, my strength. The LORD is my rock and my fortress and my deliverer; My God, my strength in whom I will trust; My shield and the horn of my salvation; my stronghold. I will call upon the LORD who is worthy to be praised; So shall I be saved from my enemies" (Psalms 18:1-3, NKJV; see also 2 Samuel 22:3).

How Jesus fulfilled

Jesus is the true commander of the army of God (Revelation 19:11-16). When Zacharias learned that the Messiah was to be born, he prophesied these words concerning Him: "Blessed is the Lord of Israel, For He has visited and redeemed His people, And has raised up a horn of salvation for us in the house of His servant David, As he spoke by the mouth of his holy prophets, Who have been since the world began, That we should be saved from our enemies and from the hand of all who hate us" (Luke 1:68-71, NKJV).

Zacharias referred to Messiah Jesus as the horn of salvation who would save them from their enemies. In the first century, the enemy that the Jews wanted to be saved from was Rome. The Jews were looking for a deliverer who would overthrow the Roman empire and establish the kingdom of David. Yet in His first coming, Jesus' purpose was not to destroy the Roman empire. His purpose was to destroy the works of Satan and the sin in men's hearts that made possible the evil and oppression of Rome.

As the Commander of the army of God and the horn of our salvation, Jesus has defeated the enemies of our soul. But His victory was not an easy one. Satan didn't give up without a fight. There was a great spiritual battle involved.

Immediately after Jesus was filled with the Holy Spirit, He encountered spiritual warfare. As Jesus drew near to God in preparation for His ministry, Satan came to tempt Him. Yet Jesus overcame Satan's temptations.

Paul says that Jesus disarmed or spoiled principalities and powers (Satan and his army) and triumphed over them (Colossians 2:15). The word spoiled means to carry off as a captive. It refers to an ancient military practice. When a general conquered his enemy, a great homecoming parade would be given in his honor. This was called the parade of triumph. When the general came into the city, he would strip the opposing king whom he had taken captive, of all his armor and march him down the main street as part of the parade. The whole city would turn out for the parade to cheer the general and celebrate the victory. They then gave him the keys to the city.

By His death and resurrection, Jesus has disarmed Satan and taken him captive. When He returned to heaven, God the Father had prepared a big homecoming parade for Him. It was the great parade of triumph. All the angels of heaven came out to meet Jesus. They cheered Him by singing, "Worthy is the Lamb who was slain to receive power and riches and wisdom, And strength and honor and glory and blessing!" (Revelation 5:12, NKJV). Then God the Father gave Jesus the key to death and hades (Revelation 1:18).

Paul wrote to the Ephesians that God the Father has given Jesus a position "far above all principality, and power, and might, and dominion, and every name that is named, not only in this world, but also in that which is to come: and hath put all things under his feet" (Ephesians 1:22-23, KJV).

He wrote to the Philippians, "Therefore God also has highly exalted Him and given Him the name which is above every name, that at the name of Jesus every knee should bow, of those in heaven, and of those on earth, and of those under the earth, and that every tongue should confess that Jesus Christ is Lord, to the glory of God the Father" (Philippians 2:9-11, NKJV).

Peter writes of Jesus, "who has gone into heaven and is at the right hand of God, angels and authorities and powers having been made subject to Him" (1 Peter 3:22, NKJV).

Jesus apparently offered a physical kingdom to the Jews as well as a spiritual one. But the physical kingdom could only be established if the Jews also accepted the spiritual one. They didn't like the kind of offer Jesus made, so they rejected Him as their king. Jesus then offered the spiritual blessings of the kingdom of God to the Gentiles. Today, every individual Jew and Gentile who accepts His offer becomes part of a new body of people called the Church. The Church presently lives in the spiritual realm of the kingdom of God.

When God completes His time of forming the Church, He will once again offer a physical, literal kingdom to the Jews as a nation. The Jews will accept God's offer and acknowledge Jesus as their King. Jesus will then return to earth and defeat the enemy nations who will be seeking to destroy the Jews. Then God Himself will rule as King over all the earth through Messiah Jesus. Both the kingdom of God and the kingdom of David will be united in His rule.

Personal application

You've probably already figured out that the Feast of Trumpets relates to the Christian's spiritual warfare. Once we experience the reality of the Feast of Pentecost and are filled with the Spirit, we too will experience spiritual warfare just as Jesus did. The closer we draw near to God, the more our spiritual battles intensify. We become a threat to Satan when we begin to walk in the power of God. He will do anything he can to defeat us. Learning how to live in the victory of Jesus Christ as the horn of salvation is a prerequisite to entering the rest of God. Thus, the Feast of Trumpets symbolizes the fifth step in our Christian walk.

Paul identifies our real enemy with these words, "Finally, my brethren, be strong in the Lord and in the power of His might. Put on the whole armor of God, that you may be able to stand against the wiles of the devil. For we wrestle not against flesh and blood, but against principalities, against powers, against the rulers of darkness of this age, against spiritual wickedness in heavenly places" (Ephesians 6:10-12, NKJV).

Paul tells us that our real enemy is the devil and a great host of demon followers that make up his army. Jesus has defeated the devil! Our strength and power comes from God through Christ as the trumpet of God. Paul said it this way to the Corinthians, "For though we walk in the flesh, we do not war according to the flesh. For the weapons of our warfare are not carnal but mighty through God for pulling down strongholds" (2 Corinthians 10:3-4, NKJV).

God has defeated Satan for us through Jesus Christ. So we don't have to defeat the devil ourselves. We simply stand in the victory God has already won for us. We do this by putting on the armor of God. Paul describes this armor for us. He writes, "Therefore take up the whole armor of God, that you may be able to withstand in the evil day, and having done all, to stand. Stand therefore, having girded your waist with truth, having put on the breastplate of righteousness and having shod your feet with the preparation of the gospel of peace; above all, taking the shield of faith with which you will be able to quench all the fiery darts of the wicked one. And take the helmet of salvation, and the sword of the Spirit, which is the word of God; praying always with all prayer and supplication in the Spirit, being watchful to this end with all perseverance and supplication for all the saints" (Ephesians 6:13-18, NKJV).

Paul mentions six pieces of armor. Each piece of armor represents an aspect of Christ Himself as the trumpet of God. Taken as a whole, they give us a symbolic description of the person and completed work of Jesus in defeating Satan for us. Here's how Paul expressed this point to the Romans, "But put on the Lord Jesus Christ, and make no provision for the flesh, to fulfill its lust" (Romans 13:14, NKJV).

Jesus Himself is our armor. He is our armor because He has defeated Satan. His victory becomes ours as we allow Him to live His life through us. The Christian's armor is simply Christ in us, living His life out of us with the result being that His victory over Satan becomes ours. This armor, as a description of Christ, shows us how to allow Christ to appropriate His victory for us in our everyday lives as we live in the power of God. Learning how to wear our armor is a necessary step to entering the rest of God. For further details on the armor and how to wear it, I suggest you read my book, *Seated in Heavenly Places* (Bridge Publishing, Inc., 1986).

Seasonal aspect

The Feast of Tabernacles, consisting of Trumpets, Atonement, and Tabernacles, is the only one of three feast seasons that has not yet been literally fulfilled in history. Both the feasts of Passover and Pentecost literally happened as were discussed in earlier chapters. There is no reason for us to believe that the Feast of Tabernacles will not also be literally fulfilled in the future. In fact, we most definitely believe that it will.

The seasonal aspect of the Feast of Tabernacles relates to the end-time events recorded in the book of Revelation.

In fact, the entire book of Revelation may be studied in light of the Feast of Tabernacles.

The book of Revelation opens up with the apostle John hearing the voice of Jesus which John likens to the sound of a trumpet. John writes, "I was in the Spirit on the Lord's Day, and I heard behind me a loud voice, as of a trumpet" (Revelation 1:10, NKJV). Isn't that interesting?

Then we notice that the first three chapters of the book of Revelation cover the period of time which we have identified as the church age. We realize this because it is these chapters that give a description of Jesus in the midst of the Church and record His letters to the seven churches.

As we progress further into the book of Revelation, we begin to see the literal fulfillment of the Feast of Trumpets. Remember that in the tenth chapter of Numbers, God instructed the Hebrews to make two silver trumpets. In the Bible, silver is symbolic of redemption. These two silver trumpets made from the same source of silver were symbolic of the Jews and the Church, both of which are redeemed by Jesus.

As the trumpets were used for different purposes, so God has different purposes for the Church and the nation of Israel. One use of the trumpets was to call the people to break camp and move out. This use of the trumpets finds its literal fulfillment in the rapture of the Church which is described in Revelation 4 and 5.

John writes, "After these things I looked, and behold, a door standing open in heaven. And the first voice which I heard was like a trumpet speaking to me, saying, 'Come up here, and I will show you things which must take place after this' " (Revelation 4:1, NKJV).

The use of the trumpets to sound an alarm for warfare finds its literal fulfillment in the restoration of the nation of Israel and the seven year tribulation period described in Revelation 6-18.

The Old Testament prophets described this period in terms of the blowing of trumpets for warfare. Joel wrote "Blow the trumpet in Zion, and sound an alarm in My holy mountain! Let all the inhabitants of the land tremble; for the day of the LORD is coming, for it is at hand" (Joel 2:1, NKJV).

Zephaniah added, "The great day of the Lord is near, It is near and hastens quickly. The noise of the day of the Lord is bitter, There the mighty men shall cry out. That day is a day of wrath, A day of trouble and distress, A day of devastation and desolation, A day of darkness and gloominess, A day of clouds and thick darkness, A day of trumpet and alarm Against the fortified cities and against the high towers. I will bring distress upon men, And they shall walk like blind men, Because they have sinned against the Lord; Their blood shall be poured out like dust, and their flesh like refuse. Neither their silver nor their gold shall be able to deliver them in the day of the Lord's wrath; but the whole land shall be devoured by the fire of His jealousy, for He will make speedy riddance of all those who dwell in the land" (Zephaniah 1:14-18, NKJV).

The ultimate fulfillment of the Feast of Trumpets is the second coming of Jesus Christ which is described in Revelation 19. It too is announced by the use of trumpets. John writes, "Then the seventh angel blew his trumpet, and there were loud voices in heaven saying, 'The kingdom of the world has become the kingdom of our Lord and of his Christ, and he shall reign for ever and ever' " (Revelation 11:15, RSV).

John goes on to say that when Jesus returns He will be coming to make war (Revelation 19:11). He will crush all of His enemies and rule with a rod of iron over a kingdom that will never end. Yes, Jesus Christ is the trumpet of God and the horn of our salvation.

Chapter Six
Review Exercise

1. Describe how Jesus fulfills the Feast of Trumpets.

2. How does the Feast of Trumpets through Jesus apply to our lives today?

3. Describe the seasonal aspect of the Feast of Trumpets.

7

atonement

One aspect of the Christian life that keeps many believers from entering God's rest is knowing how to cope with trials. We all experience difficulties which try our faith and test our obedience to the revealed will of God for our lives. How we respond to these trials often can make the difference in whether or not we ever know the rest of God. The Day of Atonement is a visual aid God has given us to teach us about our Lord Jesus Christ and how to handle the inevitable trials that confront every believer. It represents the sixth step in our walk with God.

Historical background

We read in Leviticus the following instructions concerning the Day of Atonement, "And the Lord spoke to Moses, saying: 'Also the tenth day of this seventh month shall be the Day of Atonement. It shall be a holy convocation for you; you shall afflict your souls, and offer an offering made by fire to the Lord. And you shall do no work on that same day, for it is the Day of Atonement, to make atonement for you before the Lord your God. For any person who is not afflicted of soul on that same day, he shall be cut off from his people. And any person who does any work on that same day, that person I will destroy from among his people. You shall do no manner of work; it shall be a statute forever throughout your generations in all your dwellings. It shall be to you a sabbath of solemn rest, and you shall afflict your souls; on the ninth day of the month at evening, from evening to evening, you shall celebrate your sabbath' " (Leviticus 23:26-32, NKJV).

We learn from these instructions and note on the chart that the Day of Atonement was on the tenth day of the month of Tishri. This was the great day of national cleansing and repentance from sin. It was on this day that God judged the sins of the entire nation. In view of this, the Day of Atonement became known as the Day of Judgment.

The Day of Atonement was the one day in the year when the High Priest would go behind the veil into the Holy of Holies with the blood of the sacrifice and sprinkle it on the Mercy Seat. This offering of the innocent substitutionary sacrifice made possible the atonement for the sins of the nation. The word atonement means "to cover." On the great Day of Atonement, the sins of the nation were covered by the blood of the sacrifice. This procedure is described in detail in Leviticus 16 and in my book, *The Miracle of the Scarlet Thread* (Bridge Publishing, Inc. 1981).

Because this was the Day of Judgment, it was a time of great soul affliction. It was a day of godly sorrow, godly repentance, and confession of sins. It was a time of mourning before God with a broken spirit and contrite heart. It is the only required day of fasting in the Bible. Anyone who would not repent of his sins would suffer death.

The Jews further believed that the day of final judgment and accounting of the soul would come on the Day of Atonement. On this day, the future of every individual would be sealed and the gates of heaven would be closed. In light of this belief, the Jews performed many good deeds during the ten days between the Feast of Trumpets and the Day of Atonement. This ten day period became known as the "Awesome Days" or the "Ten Days of Repentance" as the people prepared themselves spiritually for the Day of Atonement. They would express their concern and hope by greeting each other with the phrase, "may your name be inscribed in the Book of Life."

How Jesus fulfilled

Jesus fulfilled the spiritual aspects of the Day of Atonement when He went into the heavenly holy of holies with His own blood which He shed for the sins of the world. We have been forgiven and made clean once and for all by the blood of Jesus Christ. The blood of Jesus did what the blood of bulls and goats could never do. It didn't just cover our sins, it took them away to be remembered no more.

We receive this great blessing of forgiveness once and for all when we repent of our sins and, with a broken and contrite spirit, accept Jesus Christ as the innocent substitutionary sacrifice who died in our place. At that moment, our future is sealed by the Holy Spirit and our names are inscribed (recorded) in the Lamb's Book of Life. This is a finished work of redemption and salvation regarding our position before God.

Even though God has forgiven us of our sins, this does not mean that we do not need a continuous cleansing in our daily lives. We must judge our sins daily for the purpose of maintaining fellowship with our Lord. John spoke of this need with the following words, "If we say that we have fellowship with Him, and walk in darkness, we lie and do not practice the truth. But if we walk in the light as He is in the light, we have fellowship with one another, and the blood of Jesus Christ His Son cleanses us from all sin. If we say that we have no sin, we deceive ourselves, and the truth is not in us. If we confess our sins, He is faithful and just to forgive us our sins and to cleanse us from all unrighteousness" (1 John 1:6-9, NKJV).

One of the ways that God works this in us is through the trials of life that test our faith and draw us closer to God. God uses these trials to purify our motives and actions so that we might be more and more conformed to the moral character of Jesus Christ.

Jesus Himself experienced great trials. These were not for the purpose of cleansing and purifying Him because Jesus did not need this. He was perfect. His trials were tests of obedience that forced Him to constantly rely on His heavenly Father and seek Him through prayer and fasting.

Jesus purifies His bride, the Church, by baptizing us in the fiery trials of our faith. The purpose is to force us to earnestly seek God through prayer and fasting, just as He did. When John spoke of Jesus as the baptizer in the Holy Spirit, he also said that Jesus would baptize us with fire. John stated, ". . . I indeed baptize you with water; but One mightier than I is coming, whose sandal strap I am not worthy to loose. He will baptize you with the Holy Spirit and fire. His winnowing fan is in His hand, and He will thoroughly purge His threshing floor, and gather the wheat into His barn; but the chaff He will burn with unquenchable fire" (Luke 3:16-17, NKJV).

Jesus experienced this baptism in fire and promised that all who would follow Him would do likewise. We learn this from a conversation Jesus had with the mother of two of His disciples: "Then the mother of Zebedee's sons came to Him with her sons, kneeling down and asking something from Him. And He said to her, 'What do you wish?' She said to Him, 'Grant that these two sons of mine may sit, one on Your right hand and the other on the left, in Your kingdom.' But Jesus answered and said, 'You do not know what you ask. Are you able to drink the cup that I am about to drink, and be baptized with the baptism that I am baptized with?' They said to Him, 'We are able.' So He said to them, 'You will indeed drink My cup, and be baptized with the baptism that I am baptized with; but to sit on My right hand and on My left is not Mine to give, but is for those for whom it is prepared by My Father' " (Matthew 20:20-23, NKJV).

This woman wanted her two sons, James and John, to have the highest positions in Jesus' kingdom. But she was not aware of the price one must pay for such honor. Jesus said the price was to drink from the cup of baptism which He was to drink from. This cup was the great trial and testing He experienced a short time later as well as the suffering He was to endure on the cross as He became our sin bearer and was separated from the heavenly Father.

Just before His arrest, Jesus had gone to the Garden of Gethesemane to pray. This was to be His greatest time of trial and testing. As He contemplated going to the cross and being separated from His heavenly Father, His soul became greatly distressed. He took Peter, James, and John with Him hoping they would comfort Him.

He even said to them, " 'My soul is exceedingly sorrowful, even to death. Stay here and watch with Me' " (Matthew 26:38, NKJV). Then Jesus went a littler further by Himself and began to cry out to God, " 'O My Father, if it is possible, let this cup pass from Me; nevertheless, not as I will, but as You will' " (Matthew 26:39, NKJV).

This was such a heavy trial for Jesus that, in His agony, He sweat great drops of blood (Luke 22:44). He cried out in desperation for God the Father to take the cup from Him, knowing all along this was not possible. Finally, He acknowledged the Father's will for His life and surrendered in total obedience to it. Jesus then went on to give His life in fulfillment of the spiritual reality of the Day of Atonement.

Personal application

Whatever Jesus experienced in His flesh while on earth, we who are His followers will experience in our inner self. Jesus was crucified for our sins. Our response to this is to die to our self and take up our cross and follow Him. Jesus was buried with our sins. Our response is to put off the old man of sin. Jesus was raised from the dead. Likewise, we were dead in our trespasses and sins but have been raised from our spiritual grave to put on the new man and walk in newness of life.

Jesus was filled with the Holy Spirit enabling Him to minister in the power of God. We too must be filled with the Holy Spirit for the same purpose. After Jesus was filled with the Holy Spirit, He immediately encountered spiritual warfare and many trials to test His faith. When we become filled with the Holy Spirit, we also encounter spiritual warfare and great trials beyond any dimension we've ever experienced before.

Sometimes when people become Christians, they are led to believe they will, in a sense, "ride off into the sunset" with Jesus and never again have any problems. When the inevitable trials do come their way, they have not been prepared and don't know how to respond to them.

As long as we are on this planet, until Jesus returns, we are going to have trials. God uses them to keep us humble before Him, to test our faith, and to show us the real condition of our hearts. Moses understood this and said to the Jewish people, "And you shall remember that the LORD your God led you all the way these forty years in the wilderness, to humble you and test you, to know what was in your heart, whether you would keep His commandments or not" (Deuteronomy 8:2, NKJV).

Peter spoke of this with these words, "Beloved, do not think it strange concerning the fiery trial which is to try you, as though some strange thing happened to you . . . For the time has come for judgement to begin at the house of God . . . Therefore let those who suffer according to the will of God commit their souls to Him in doing good, as to a faithful Creator" (1 Peter 4:12, 17, 19, NKJV).

Jesus did not die to save us from trials and problems. He died in order that we might have victory and God's rest in spite of our trials and problems while going through them. Our response to trials is not to run from them or pretend they don't exist, but to commit our soul to God who, as our faithful Creator, will never allow us to have a trial so great that He will not give us the grace to handle it victoriously (see 1 Corinthians 10:13; 2 Corinthians 12:9-10). My intent here is not to debate whether God actually causes trials or merely allows them, but rather to point out their obvious existence and provide some help in coping with them.

Once again, we turn to Peter for instruction on this subject. He says, "In this you greatly rejoice, though now for a little while, if need be, you have been grieved by various trials, that the genuineness of your faith, being much more precious than gold that perishes, though it be tested by fire, may be found to praise, honor and glory at the revelation of Jesus Christ" (1 Peter 1:7-8, NKJV).

We see several important points in the statement by Peter that should help us better cope with trials and difficult circumstances. First of all, he says we will only have a trial *"if need be."* In other words, God will not allow us to experience a difficult trial of our faith unless He sees some value in it for our life. There is a purpose in every trial we face. The overall purpose, as previously stated, is to purify our motives and actions so we might be more like Jesus. Therefore, when experiencing a trial, we should take our eyes off the circumstances and try to view the situation from an eternal perspective.

Peter next encourages us by saying any trial we must face will be only for *"a little while."* It won't last forever. Once God has used it to accomplish His purpose in our life, the trial will pass. We determine how long the trial will last by the way we respond to it. If we become angry with God because of our trial, or try to run from it, we actually prolong it. But if we seek God through prayer and fasting with a broken and contrite spirit, the trial will quickly pass.

Peter then states that we will have *"various"* trials. Sometimes it seems that our whole world is falling apart; that everything seems to be going wrong. This does not necessarily mean you are living in sin or that God is trying to punish you. It could very well be just the normal pressures of life that pile up on us from time to time. God will use them in your life to develop His character in you, if you'll let Him do so.

Next, Peter points out that going through a trial can be a very grevious and stressful experience. To acknowledge this does not mean that we lack faith, or that we're not trusting God. It merely means we're facing the situation realistically and "telling it like it is." In other words, we're being human and honest. But we do not have to carry this burden alone. Instead, we give our burden to God through prayer and thanksgiving (1 Peter 5:7).

Peter finally states that the purpose of trials is to test the genuineness of our faith. He compares this test to the process used in purifying gold. When a miner finds gold, the ore contains a lot of impurities. The miner must "test" the gold for the purpose of separating it from the impurities. The way he does this is to put the gold in a crucible which he places over a fiery furnace. The heat from the fire causes the impurities to rise to the top of the crucible. The miner then skims off the impurities and looks down into the material in the crucible. He cannot see if there is more impure material because it will be at the bottom of the crucible.

But, if he cannot see a clear reflection of his image, he knows there are more impurities at the bottom that need to be removed. The way he removes them is by turning up the fire. This causes more impurities to rise to the top, and once again, the miner skims them off. He repeats this process until he is able to see a clear reflection of his image in the remaining material in the crucible. At this point he knows he has separated out all the impurities.

This illustration helps us to understand why we have trials and how God uses them to test our faith. The Old Testament prophets spoke of God as a refiner who would burn out the moral and spiritual impurities from our lives. Malachi said, "He will sit as a refiner and a purifier of silver; He will purge the sons of Levi, And purge them as gold and silver, That they offer to the LORD an offering in righteousness" (Malachi 3:5, NKJV). (See also Isaiah 1:25.)

God desires that we, His children, be conformed to His image. So like the old miner, He tests our faith. He uses the trials of life for the purpose of bringing to the top of our attention, those things hidden deep down in our hearts below the surface, which we do not even know are there. Then He skims them off through our prayers, praise, and if necessary, repentance. He repeats this process, making the fiery trial hotter if necessary, until there is nothing left of us—but Him.

Job was a man who suffered great trials. But he found comfort in knowing that God was working in his life. Job understood the refining process God often allows us to experience and said, "Look, I go forward, but He is not there, And backward, but I cannot perceive Him; When He works on the left hand, I cannot behold Him; When He turns to the right hand, I cannot see Him. But He knows the way that I take; When He has tested me, I shall come forth as gold" (Job 23:8-10, NKJV).

You may be going through a trial. Perhaps you cannot sense God's presence, but He *is* there. He promised never to leave you nor forsake you (Hebrews 13:5). God says to you, "When you pass through the waters, I will be with you; And through the rivers, they shall not overflow you. When you walk through the fire, you shall not be burned, Nor shall the flame scorch you" (Isaiah 43:2, NKJV).

God knows the way that you take. He knows what's going on in your life. He knows what is best for you from an eternal perspective. He knows what you can handle and what you can't. He knows what He's doing in your life. Take comfort in these words, "When He has tried you, you shall come forth as gold."

This leads us to the final point which Peter makes concerning our response to trials. He says, of all things, we should rejoice in them. The reason we can rejoice in a trial is because God uses it for His glory and our good. The good for which He uses it is to make us more like Him so that our very lives will be an offering in righteousness.

Seasonal aspect

Seasonally, the Day of Atonement points to the return of Jesus Christ to judge the sins of the world. As noted on the chart, this is a future event that will be the literal fulfillment of the final great Day of Atonement.

God established in the Jewish administration of time, every fiftieth year as a Year of Jubilee (Leviticus 27). This was a special year when all the prisoners were set free, property was returned to its original owner and the land rested, without being worked. This was the year for proclaiming liberty throughout the land. It was a time of great rejoicing.

The Year of Jubilee begins on the Day of Atonement. It points to the great Year of Jubilee when Jesus Christ will come to earth to judge the world. Then, God's people will be set free once and for all from the trials of life. The rule of earth will be restored to the godly and there will be rest in the land. This will be a day of mourning for those who will be judged but a day of rejoicing for we who have been waiting for Christ's return.

The prophet Zechariah was speaking of the future literal fulfillment of the Day of Atonement when he wrote, "And I will pour on the house of David and on the inhabitants of Jerusalem the Spirit of grace and supplication; then they will look on Me whom they have pierced; they will mourn for Him as one mourns for his only son, and grieve for Him as one grieves for a firstborn. In that day there shall be a great mourning in Jerusalem, like the mourning at Hadad Rimmon in the plain of Megiddo. And the land shall mourn, every family by itself, and their wives by themselves; the family of Nathan by itself, and their wives by themselves; the family of the house of Levi by itself, and their wives by themselves; the family of Shimei by itself, and their wives by themselves; all the families that remain, every family by itself, and their wives by themselves" (Zechariah 12:10-14, NKJV).

Zechariah then added this further word, " 'In that day a fountain shall be opened for the house of David and for the inhabitants of Jerusalem, for sin and for uncleanness. It shall be in that day,' says the Lord of hosts, 'that I will cut off the names of the idols from the land, and they shall no longer be remembered. I will also cause the prophets and the unclean spirit to depart from the land. And it shall come to pass in all the land,' says the Lord, 'That two-thirds in it shall be cut off and die, But one third shall be left in it: I will bring the one-third through the fire, will refine them as silver is refined, And test them as gold is tested. They will call on My name, And I will answer them. I will say, "This is My people"; And each one will say, "The Lord is my God" ' " (Zechariah 13:1-2, 8-9, NKJV).

Jesus also referred to this time when speaking about His second coming. He said, "Immediately after the tribulation of those days the sun will be darkened, and the moon will not give its light; the stars will fall from heaven, and the powers of the heavens will be shaken. Then the sign of the Son of Man will appear in heaven, and then all the tribes of the earth will mourn, and they will see the Son of Man coming on the clouds of heaven with power and great glory. And He will send His angels with a great sound of a trumpet, and they will gather together His elect from the four winds; from one end of heaven to the other" (Matthew 24:29-31, NKJV).

John said these words in the book of Revelation, "Behold He is coming with clouds, and every eye will see Him, and they also who pierced Him. And all the tribes of the earth will mourn because of Him. Even so, Amen" (Revelation 1:7, NKJV).

John had the great privilege of writing about Jesus' literal fulfillment of the Day of Atonement. He writes, "Then I saw heaven opened, and behold, a white horse. And He who sat on him was called Faithful and True, and in righteousness He judges and makes war. His eyes were like a flame of fire, and on His head were many crowns. He had a name written that no one knew except Himself. He was clothed with a robe dipped in blood, and His name is called the Word of God. And the armies in heaven, clothed in fine linen, white and clean, followed Him on white horses. Now out of His mouth goes a sharp sword that with it He should strike the nations. And He Himself will rule them with a rod of iron. He Himself treads the winepress of the fierceness and wrath of Almighty God. And He has on His robe and on His thigh a name written: KING OF LORDS, AND LORD OF LORDS" (Revelation 19:11-16, NKJV).

Chapter Seven
Review Exercise

1. Describe how Jesus fulfills the Feast of Atonement.

2. How does the Feast of Atonement through Jesus apply to our lives today?

3. Describe the seasonal aspect of the Feast of Atonement.

8

tabernacles

The last feast that God gave the Hebrews to observe was the Feast of Tabernacles. It was also called the Feast of Ingathering because it was at the end of the harvest season and the Feasts of Booths because the Hebrews slept in booths or shelters during the feast (Exodus 23:16; Deuteronomy 16:16).

The Feast of Tabernacles celebrated the final ingathering of the harvest God had blessed the people with for the year. The fruit of the land had been reaped so the people could now rest from their harvest labors. Therefore, it was a time of great rejoicing. It was such a joyous occasion that the Jews said the person who had not been to Jerusalem during the Feast of Tabernacles just didn't know what rejoicing really meant!

Because the Feast of Tabernacles was the last of the seven feasts, it completed the religious season. The number seven in the Bible represents completion. We learn from this that the Feast of Tabernacles represents the completed or finished work of God in both this present age in which we live and the lives of individual Christians. Thus it corresponds to the seventh step in our walk with God to reach spiritual maturity and rest in our souls. This is not the same as sinless perfection. We never will achieve this until Jesus returns. It is, however, a level of maturity to which we can grow, whereby we have learned to rest in God for who He is and be content in whatever circumstances we find ourselves. The apostle Paul recognized this condition in his own life. He was not perfect but he had matured to a place of rest in God. He wrote of this work of God in his life to the Philippians and said, "Not that I have already attained, or am already perfected; but I press on, that I may lay hold of that for which Christ Jesus has also laid hold of me. Brethren, I do not count myself to have apprehended; but one thing I do, forgetting those things which are behind and reaching forward to those things which are ahead, I press toward the goal for the prize of the upward call of God in Christ Jesus. . . . Not that I speak in regard to need, for I have learned in whatever state I am, to be content: I know how to be abased, and I know how to abound. Everywhere and in all things I have learned both to be full and to be hungry, both to abound and to suffer need. I can do all things through Christ who strengthens me" (Philippians 3:12-14; 4:11-13, NKJV).

Historical background

Let's now read the instructions God gave the Jews concerning the Feast of Tabernacles. Leviticus says, "Then the Lord spoke to Moses saying, 'Speak to the children of Israel, saying, "The fifteenth day of this seventh month shall be the Feast of Tabernacles for seven days to the Lord. On the first day there shall be a holy convocation. You shall do no customary work on it. For seven days you shall offer an offering made by fire to the Lord. On the eighth day you shall have a holy convocation, and you shall offer an offering made by fire to the Lord. It is a sacred assembly, and you shall do no customary work on it" ' " (Leviticus 23:33-36, NKJV).

God then repeats the command and gives further instructions, " ' "Also on the fifteenth day of the seventh month, when you have gathered in the fruit of the land, you shall keep the feast of the Lord for seven days; on the first day there shall be a sabbath-rest, and on the eighth day a sabbath-rest. And you shall take for yourselves on the first day the fruit of beautiful trees, branches of palm trees, the boughs of leafy trees, and willows of the brook, and you shall rejoice before the Lord your God for seven days. You shall keep it as a feast to the Lord for seven days in the year. It shall be a statute forever in your generations. You shall celebrate it in the seventh month. You shall dwell in booths for seven days. All who are native Israelites shall dwell in booths, that your generations may know that I made the children of Israel dwell in booths when I brought them out of the land of Egypt: I am the Lord your God" ' " (verses 39-43, NKJV) (see also Numbers 29 for a description of sacrifices that were offered at this feast).

We learn from this text and note on the chart that the Feast of Tabernacles began on the fifteenth of Tishri and lasted through the twenty-first. Then on the twenty-second (the eighth day), there was a special Sabbath which was a day of rest characterized by much rejoicing.

The Feast of Tabernacles had two aspects associated with it. First, it looked back to the forty years when the Jews wandered in the wilderness desert living in shelters or tabernacles. They were always to be reminded that the wanderings of their forefathers were brought about by unbelief and disobedience, but they were only temporary. Yet, during their wanderings, God was in their midst providing for their every need and eventually brought them into the land of rest He had promised them.

As a constant reminder of all of this, God commanded the Hebrews to build booths or shelters to live in during this feast. So every year at the Feast of Tabernacles, the Hebrews would gather the necessary wood and branches and build a shelter in which they would live during the feast.

But the Feast of Tabernacles also had a forward look. The shelter was loosely constructed so that the Hebrews could see through its roof into heaven. This would remind them that they were pilgrims passing through this life and that God had an even greater rest for them in the future when He would come and live among them permanently.

The final rest was the hope of their ancestor Abraham. The writer of Hebrews referred to this and said, "By faith Abraham obeyed when he was called to go out to a place which he was to receive an inheritance; and he went out, not knowing where he was to go. By faith he sojourned in the land of promise, as in a foreign land, living in tents with Isaac and Jacob, heirs with him of the same promise. For he looked forward to the city which has foundations, whose builder and maker is God" (Hebrews 11:8-10, RSV).

How Jesus fulfilled

Jesus Christ is the tabernacle or dwelling place of God. In Him dwelled all the fullness of God (John 1:14; Colossians 2:9) and God dwells in our midst through Jesus Christ (Matthew 18:20). Jesus will ultimately fulfill the Feast of Tabernacles at His second coming. There will be a literal rest for planet earth and all its inhabitants. Until then, we can know His rest in our souls.

On one occasion Jesus said, "Come to Me, all you who labor and are heavy laden, and I will give you rest. Take My yoke upon you and learn from Me, for I am gentle and lowly in heart, and you will find rest for your souls. For My yoke is easy and My burden is light" (Matthew 11:28-30, NKJV).

Jesus claimed that we could find rest in God through Him. Many Christians seek God's rest by working for God or

---

trying to get something from God. But God, through a personal relationship with Jesus Christ, is our rest. Jesus doesn't give us life; He *is* our life. He doesn't give us health; He *is* our health. He doesn't give us the fruit and gifts of the Spirit; He *is* the fruit and gifts of the Spirit. These are simply manifestations of His own life.

Many Christians never enter God's rest because they're seeking things from Jesus rather than Jesus Himself. They seek blessings rather than the Blesser. Jesus doesn't give us blessings; He Himself is our blessing. He is all that we could ever need, want, or hope for. He is our rest. His rest is available for us when we allow Him to fully dwell in our midst as Lord and master of our soul. This becomes a reality to us by the Holy Spirit, through whom the life of Christ flows to us and through us.

There were two Jewish rituals associated with the Feast of Tabernacles that dramatically illustrated the difference between seeking things *from* God rather than seeking God. Jesus claimed that both of these rituals pointed to Himself.

The first was the ritual of the pouring of water. This took place on the last day of the Feast of Tabernacles. This day was called in Hebrew *Hoshana Rabba* which means the "Day of Great Hosanna." This Hebrew phrase translates into English as the words "save now." The Day of the Great Hosanna was the day when the Jews would pray particularly for God's salvation through the Messiah. The ritual of the pouring of water had both a physical and spiritual significance. The rainy season was about to begin (see calendar), and the Jews needed the rain to soften the ground for plowing. In view of this, they made a special thanksgiving offering to God for the rain He was going to send. The spiritual significance, as just mentioned, pointed to the coming of the Messiah who would give them the living waters of His Spirit.

As part of the ritual proceeding, a certain priest would draw water from the Pool of Siloam with a golden pitcher. He would then come to the altar at the Temple where the High Priest would take the pitcher and pour the water into a basin at the foot of the altar.

As this was taking place, the priests blew their trumpets, and the Levites and all the people waved palm branches while singing from Psalms 113-118. About the time the water was being poured they were singing, "Save now, I pray, O LORD; O LORD, I pray, send now prosperity. Blessed is he who comes in the name of the LORD" (Psalms 118:25-26, NKJV).

This was the most joyous day of the celebration and the pouring of the water was the most joyous moment of the day. Jesus was there to keep the feast in obedience to the law. Just as the fervor of the celebration reaches its peak at the pouring of the water, Jesus makes a bold declaration. John was an eyewitness to it and wrote, "On the last day, the great day of the feast, Jesus stood and cried out, saying, 'If anyone thirsts, let him come to Me and drink. He who believes in Me, as the Scripture has said, out of his heart will flow rivers of living water.' But this He spoke concerning the Spirit, whom those believing in Him would receive; for the Holy Spirit was not yet given, because Jesus was not yet glorified" (John 7:37-39, NKJV).

With this statement Jesus was saying, "Look unto me and be saved now. I am the great hosanna. I am your salvation. I will give the living waters of the Holy Spirit to all who will receive me as the tabernacle of God."

The other ritual was the lighting of the Temple. Tens of thousands of pilgrims who had come to Jerusalem to keep the feast crowded into the Temple area, each one carrying a lighted torch. The entire city was illuminated for miles. This too had a physical and spiritual significance. Plenty of sunshine was needed along with the rain to have a successful agricultural season. The Jews thanked God for the sun that was necessary for the life of the harvest. They also acknowledged that God Himself was the true light (Psalms 27:1) who would give them spiritual life through the Messiah.

It was during this occasion that Jesus made another bold statement that most assuredly got their attention. John records it for us, "Then Jesus spoke to them again, saying, 'I am the light of the world. He who follows Me shall not walk in darkness, but have the light of life' " (John 8:12, NKJV).

At both of these very special festival events, Jesus proclaimed in a clear and powerful way that He was the reality to which they pointed. He had come to satisfy their spiritual thirst and give them spiritual life. Yet they rejected Him. They rejected Him for two reasons. The first reason is that they loved their religious rituals and traditions more than they loved God. And secondy, they were more interested in what God could do for them politically (deliver them from Rome) than for what he could do spiritually (deliver them from sin). The result has been that they missed the rest Jesus offered them and have been restless wanderers for the past 2,000 years, not only as a people, but in their souls as well.

Personal application

There is a rest for our souls today as well as a future heavenly rest. The writer of Hebrews explains what we must do to enter this rest. He begins by reminding us that God had a rest for the Hebrews but that they failed to embrace it. He says, "Therefore, as the Holy Spirit says: 'Today, if you will hear His voice, Do not harden your hearts as in the rebellion, In the day of trial in the wilderness, Where your fathers tested Me, proved Me, And saw My works forty years. Therefore I was angry with that generation, And said, "They always go astray in their heart, And they have not known My ways." So I swore in My wrath, "They shall not enter My rest" ' " (Hebrews 3:7-11, NKJV).

It was God's desire to lead the Hebrews into their promised land of rest. But an entire generation didn't make it. They died out in the wilderness because of unbelief and disobedience brought about by a hard heart against God.

The writer then warns us against the same problem. He says, "Beware, brethren, lest there be in any of you an evil heart of unbelief in departing from the living God; but exhort one another daily, while it is called 'Today,' lest any of you be hardened through the deceitfulness of sin. For we have become partakers of Christ if we hold the beginning of our confidence steadfast to the end, while it is said: Today, if you will hear His voice, Do not harden your hearts as in the rebellion" (verses 12-15, NKJV).

Finally, as if to press the point, we are further exhorted by another reminder, "For who, having heard, rebelled? Indeed, was it not all who came out of Egypt, led by Moses? Now with whom did He swear that they would not enter His rest, but to those who did not obey? So we see that they could not enter in because of unbelief" (verses 16-19, NKJV).

The Hebrews who came out of Egypt and died in the wilderness were saved, but they did not enter God's rest (see Numbers 14:19-23).

In the Bible, Egypt symbolizes the world system. The promised land represents God's rest. The wilderness lies in between. When a person accepts Jesus as Savior, God delivers them out of a type of spiritual Egypt. We come out of Egypt at the moment we receive Christ into our life. But Egypt (ways of the world) doesn't always come out of us, at least not for a while.

Like the Hebrews of old, we Christians will not enjoy God's rest in this life unless we walk with Him in loving trust and obedience. This involves taking the seven steps that are presented in this book. You will experience His rest in heaven, the forward look of this feast, but you will miss it in this present life.

God wants us to enter His rest right now in our soul through a daily walk with Him. The first step is to accept Jesus as the Passover lamb who died for our sins. At the moment we receive Christ into our life, we experience a spiritual birth which is so dramatic, Jesus spoke of it as being born again (John 3:1-8). We then die to our old self-life (Egypt in us) by putting off the old man and putting on the new man. These two steps are necessary to produce the character of Christ in us.

Believers who have taken these first steps are Passover Christians. They have peace with God and the peace of God. But they have not fully experienced the power of God. They must go on to the fourth step—Pentecost. The Pentecostal experience enables the believer to be an effective witness and to minister in the power of the Holy Spirit. But the Pentecostal Christian is only halfway to God's rest. He or she must go on to become tabernacle Christians. We must all learn how to conduct spiritual warfare and handle the trials of our faith. As we take each of these steps in trust and obedience to God, we will enjoy His divine rest in our souls.

Seasonal aspect

I believe the Feast of Tabernacles represents the 1,000 year reign of Jesus Christ on earth. This period of time is known as the Millennium, from the latin words *milli* (one thousand) and *annum* (year). It will be a time of great rejoicing. The results of the curse of sin will be lifted and Satan bound so that both earth and its inhabitants will enjoy the rest of God.

This 1,000 year reign of Christ is the subject of the twentieth chapter of Revelation. We read in the first six verses, "Then I saw an angel coming down from heaven, having the key to the bottomless pit and a great chain in his hand. He laid hold of the dragon, that serpent of old, who is the Devil and Satan, and bound him for a thousand years; and he cast him into the bottomless pit, and shut him up, and set a seal on him, so that he should deceive the nations no more till the thousand years were finished. But after these things he must be released for a little while. And I saw thrones, and they sat on them, and judgement was committed to them. And I saw the souls of those who had been beheaded for their witness to Jesus and for the word of God, who had not worshiped the beast or his image, and had not received his mark on their foreheads or on their hands. And they lived and reigned with Christ for a thousand years. But the rest of the dead did not live again until the thousand years were finished. This is the first resurrection" (Revelation 20:1-6, NKJV).

This seasonal rest of the Feast of Tabernacles is described in detail throughout the Bible, but particularly by the Old Testament prophets. It is the utopia for which man has so desperately strived for but never achieved.

Isaiah was looking forward to this time when He wrote, "Therefore the redeemed of the LORD shall return, and come with singing unto Zion; and everlasting joy shall be upon their head: they shall obtain gladness and joy; and sorrow and mourning shall flee away" (Isaiah 51:11, KJV).

As wonderful as this time will be for the earth and its inhabitants, it is still not the final rest that God has for us. We read in Leviticus that there was a special Sabbath on the eighth day (the twenty-second). This day was a day of great rejoicing and corresponds to the new heaven and new earth described in Revelation 21 and 22.

John writes, "And I saw a new heaven and a new earth, for the first heaven and the first earth had passed away. Also there was no more sea. Then I, John, saw the holy city, New Jerusalem, coming down out of heaven from God, prepared as a bride adorned for her husband. And I heard a loud voice from heaven saying, "Behold the tabernacle of God is with men, and He will dwell with them, and they shall be His people, and God Himself will be with them and be their God. And God will wipe away every tear from their eyes; there shall be no more death, nor sorrow, nor crying; and there shall be no more pain, for the former things have passed away. Then He who sat on the throne said, Behold I make all things new. And He said to me, Write, for these words are true and faithful. And He said to me, It is done! I am the Alpha and the Omega, the Beginning and the End. I will give of the fountain of the water of life freely to him who thirsts" (Revelation 21:1-6, NKJV).

In these verses, John says that God will transfer His home from heaven to earth. God will dwell in our midst and pull down the curtain on the closing act of human history. Then eternity will begin with God coming to live in the midst of His people. This is the final rest for which we are all waiting.

John gives this last word, "And he showed me a pure river of water of life, clear as crystal, proceeding from the throne of God and of the Lamb. In the middle of its street, and on either side of the river, was the tree of life, which bore twelve fruits, each tree yielding its fruit every month. And the leaves of the tree were for the healing of the nations. And there shall be no more curse, but the throne of God and of the Lamb shall be in it, and His servants shall serve Him. They shall see His face, and His name shall be on their foreheads. And there shall be no night there: They need no lamp nor light of the sun, for the Lord God gives them light. And they shall reign forever and ever" (Revelation 22:1-5, NKJV).

Jesus Christ alone is our peace, our power, and our rest!

Chapter Eight
Review Exercise

1. Describe how Jesus fulfills the Feast of Tabernacles.

2. How does the Feast of Tabernacles through Jesus apply to our lives today?

3. Describe the seasonal aspect of the Feast of Tabernacles.

BIBLE STUDY MATERIALS BY RICHARD BOOKER

BOOKS

For additional copies of this or other books by Richard Booker, order through your local bookstore or clip and mail the Order Form which is provided on the last page of this book following the tape list.

Richard's books can best be described as foundational books written in clear, easy-to-understand language and readable format for practical Christian living. They may be read or studied for deeper understanding of the Bible. They are primarily written for Christians of all levels of maturity but are appropriate for anyone seeking to know God. The following is a list of Richard's current books.

THE MIRACLE OF THE SCARLET THREAD

This book explains how the Old and New Testaments are woven together by the scarlet thread of the blood covenant to tell one complete story throughout the Bible.

COME AND DINE

This book takes the mystery and confusion out of the Bible. It provides background information on how we got the Bible, a survey of every book in the Bible and how each relates to Jesus Christ, practical principles, forms and guidelines for your own personal Bible study and a systematic plan for effectively reading, studying and understanding the Bible for yourself.

INTIMACY WITH GOD

This book is about the God of the Bible. It shows the ways in which God has revealed Himself to us and explains the attributes, plans and purposes of God. Then each attribute is related practically to the reader. This book takes you into the very heart of God and demonstrates how to draw near to Him.

RADICAL CHRISTIAN LIVING
This book explains how you can grow to become a mature Christian and help others do so as well. You'll learn the pathway to Christian maturity and how to select and train others in personal follow-up and disciplining at different levels of Christian growth.

SEATED IN HEAVENLY PLACES
This book helps the reader learn how to live the victorious Christian life and walk in the power of God. It explains how to minister to others, wear the armor of God and exercise spiritual authority.

BLOW THE TRUMPET IN ZION
This book explains the dramatic story of God's covenant plan for Israel including their past glory and suffering, present crisis and future hope.

JESUS IN THE FEASTS OF ISRAEL
This book is a study of the Old Testament feasts showing how they pointed to Jesus and their personal and prophetic significance for today's world. The book points out how the Feasts represent seven steps to Christian growth and the peace, power and rest of God.

BOOK ORDER FORM

Ordering Instructions

To order books, check the appropriate box, then clip and mail the coupon below to SOUNDS OF THE TRUMPET, INC., 8230 BIRCHGLENN, HOUSTON, TX 77070.

☐ Please send me _____ copy(ies) of THE MIRACLE OF THE SCARLET THREAD. I have enclosed $6.95 contribution for each copy ordered (price includes shipping).

☐ Please send me _____ copy(ies) of COME AND DINE. I have enclosed $6.95 contribution for each copy ordered (price includes shipping).

☐ Please send me _____ copy(ies) of INTIMACY WITH GOD. I have enclosed $6.95 contribution for each copy ordered (price includes shipping).

☐ Please send me _____ copy(ies) of RADICAL CHRISTIAN LIVING. I have enclosed $6.95 contribution for each copy ordered (price includes shipping).

☐ Please send me _____ copy(ies) of SEATED IN HEAVENLY PLACES. I have enclosed $6.95 contribution for each copy ordered (price includes shipping).

☐ Please send me _____ copy(ies) of BLOW THE TRUMPET IN ZION. I have enclosed $6.95 contribution for each copy ordered (price includes shipping).

☐ Please send me _____ copy(ies) of JESUS IN THE FEASTS OF ISRAEL. I have enclosed $6.95 contribution for each copy ordered (price includes shipping).

☐ Please send me a free brochure describing your workshop on how to study the Bible.

☐ Foreign order please include an extra $2.00 for surface postage.

_____

Name _____

Street _____

City _____

State _____ Zip _____

CHRISTIAN GROWTH SEMINARS

COME AND DINE
This is a one-day workshop designed for the purpose of teaching people how to study the Bible for themselves systematically. Each participant receives a 96-page workbook.

HOW TO GET YOUR PRAYERS ANSWERED
This is a one-day seminar designed for the purpose of helping Christians learn how to pray more effective and powerful prayers that will get postive results. Each participant receives an 84-page workbook.

AUDIO CASSETTE TAPE ALBUMS
A list of Richard's teaching cassettes is included on the following pages. All tape series come in an attractive album for your convenience. To order tapes, check the appropriate box, then clip and mail the Order Form which is provided on the last page of this book following the tape list.

TAPE LIST

■ *Philippians Series*

PH1	Background & Prayer
PH2	Victory In Tribulation
PH3	Keys To Unity
PH4	Honoring One Another
PH5	True Righteousness
PH6	Going On With God
PH7	Standing Together
PH8	Sufficiency Of God

■ *Colossians Series*

CO1	Background
CO2	Person & Work Of Christ
CO3	Christ In You
CO4	Sufficiency Of Christ
CO5	Christ Our Life
CO6	New Man In Christ
CO7	Christ In The Home
CO8	Christ Outside The Home

■ *Thessalonians Series*

TH1	Background & Prayer
TH2	A Winning Defense
TH3	A Welcome Report
TH4	Walking to Please God
TH5	The Day of the Lord
TH6	Background & Prayer
TH7	Day of the Lord Again
TH8	No Bums Allowed

■ *Single Messages (Circle Below)*

SM1	Why God Had To Become Man
SM2	Who Was That God Begat
SM3	Feasts Of The Lord
SM4	Philemon
SM5	Lord's Prayer
SM6	Handling Worry
SM7	Knowing God's Will
SM8	Spiritual Leprosy
SM9	Praying In The Name
SM10	Bible Baptisms
SM11	Signs Of His Coming
SM12	Times Of The Gentiles
SM13	Christian Giving
SM14	Master Theme Of Bible
SM15	The Dominant Force
SM16	Personal Testimony
SM17	Call To Discipleship
SM18	Where Are the Dead?

TAPE ORDER FORM

Ordering Instructions
To order tapes, check the appropriate box, then clip and mail the coupon below to SOUNDS OF THE TRUMPET, INC., 8230 BIRCHGLENN, HOUSTON, TX 77070.

☐ Please send me the following tapes. I have enclosed a $4.00 contribution for each tape ordered (No C.O.D.), plus $1.00 for mailing.

☐ The Bible Series	($32.00)	☐ The Feasts Series	(24.00)
☐ Getting To Know God—1	($16.00)	☐ The Sacrifices Series	($20.00)
☐ Getting To Know God—2	($20.00)	☐ Love Notes From Jesus	(28.00)
☐ Getting To Know God—3	($16.00)	☐ Ephesians Series	($48.00)
☐ Blood Covenant Series	($24.00)	☐ Philippians Series	($32.00)
☐ Abundant Life Series	($24.00)	☐ Colossians Series	($32.00)
☐ The Church Series	($24.00)	☐ Thessalonians Series	($32.00)
☐ The Christian Family	($16.00)	☐ Single Messages (Circle)	
☐ Faith & Healing Series	($12.00)	(SM1,2,3,4,5,6,7,8,9,10,	
☐ End Times Series	($32.00)	11,12,13,14,15,16,17,18)	
☐ Prayer Series	($24.00)	☐ Practical Studies—1	($24.00)
☐ Foundational Studies—1	($24.00)	☐ Practical Studies—2	($24.00)
☐ Foundational Studies—2	($24.00)		

Name _____

Street _____

City _____

State _____ Zip _____